Learn Life's Great Lesson

Your life on Earth is a *spiritual* path. Your life *is* your path. There is no other.

Some of us realize this great lesson early on. Most of us have to learn it the hard way! Either way, we all eventually come to see that the recurring painful lessons in this life are no less than part of a secret Celestial Curriculum—a course in higher consciousness designed specifically for each one of us to help us let go and realize the divine life that already dwells within us.

The path to this perfected life, to fulfilling the promise of our True Self, must be found and traveled *within*. To successfully walk it requires new and higher self-knowledge, out of which—if embraced—is born new and higher self-awareness. The higher actions that follow this self-awakening are without conflict and contradiction. Freedom appears within as well as around us. Real life is realized. At last . . . everything is as we always knew it should be.

For the sincere seeker, this book is a true source of higher self-knowledge. Within it, you will read, recognize, and realize the timeless truths you have been searching for . . . higher answers that reveal the next step for you on your way Home.

About the Author

Guy Finley is the acclaimed author of eighteen books and tape albums on the subject of self-realization and inner development, several of which have become international bestsellers. His works are widely endorsed by doctors, professionals, and religious leaders of all denominations.

His successful careers have included recording contracts at RCA and Motown records, as well as writing award-winning songs for many popular recording artists, motion pictures, and episodic TV programs. In 1979, at the age of twenty-nine, he voluntarily retired from the entertainment business and began traveling the world over in search of higher wisdom. In the last twenty years, Guy has appeared on over 400 national and local radio and TV programs, including *Coast to Coast*, *Sally Jesse Raphael*, *Entertainment Tonight*, *Michael Jackson*, and many more.

To Write to the Author

Guy Finley lives and teaches in southern Oregon. He is the founder of the Life of Learning Foundation, a nonprofit, nondenominational center for Higher Self study. He speaks at the Foundation four times each week. Everyone is welcome.

If you would like to write to the author about his book, receive information about his ongoing classes, or request a catalogue of his works (along with a free helpful study guide), send a self-addressed, stamped envelope to:

Guy Finley
Life of Learning Foundation
P.O. Box 10-S
Merlin, OR 97532
Or call (541) 476-1200 (M–Sat, 10–4 PM, PST)

For a complete list of over 100 life-healing works by Guy Finley, visit his award-winning, multimedia website at www.guyfinley.com. Log on and read or listen to excerpts from selected books and tapes. Request a free poster filled with helpful guidance. Join the free "Key Lesson" Club, and each week you'll receive an encouraging inner-life insight delivered right to your desktop via e-mail. Plus, join Guy Finley's ongoing free monthly chat room, and more!

Seeker's Guide to Self-Freedom

Truths for Living

Guy Finley

2002
Llewellyn Publications
St. Paul, Minnesota 55164-0383, U.S.A.

Special thanks to Denise Welch for her help in organizing this material

FIRST EDITION
First Printing, 2002

Cover art © Digital Stock
Cover design by Lisa Novak
Editing and book design by Rebecca Zins

Library of Congress Cataloging-in-Publication Data
Finley, Guy, 1949-
 Seeker's guide to self-freedom : truths for living / Guy Finley.—1st ed.
  p.   cm.
 ISBN 0-7387-0107-6
 1. Spiritual life.   2. Self-actualization (Psychology)   I. Title.

BL624 .F5165 2002
291.4'4—dc21

2001046291

Llewellyn Publications
A Division of Llewellyn Worldwide, Ltd.
P.O. Box 64383, Dept. 0-7387-0107-6
St. Paul, MN 55164-0383, U.S.A.
www.llewellyn.com

Printed in the United States of America

Guy Finley

is the author of more than 18 books and tape albums
on the subject of self-realization and higher success.
For a complete list of titles, visit www.guyfinley.com
or write to Life of Learning Foundation,
P.O. Box 10-S, Merlin, OR, 97532.

Other Books by Guy Finley

The Secret of Letting Go
Freedom from the Ties that Bind
The Lost Secrets of Prayer
The Intimate Enemy
Design Your Destiny

Cassette Tape Albums

Secret Teachings of the Sacred Testaments
Only the Fearless Are Free
The Road to Good Fortune
Living in the Light
7 Characteristics of Higher Consciousness
Secrets of Cleansing Your Heart, Mind, and Soul
Teachings of the Timeless Kindness
Waking Up Together

Books on Tape

The Secret of Letting Go
The Lost Secrets of Prayer

Booklets

30 Keys to Change Your Destiny
5 Steps to Complete Freedom from Stress

Video Tape Albums

Forgotten Practices for Self-Awakening
Secrets of Cleansing Your Heart, Mind, and Soul

Dedication

Seen or not, we each live in a world
The size of our understanding,
Inhabited by the creatures
Our consciousness permits,
And governed by the contents of our heart.

This explains why the wise are happy
And the ignorant so often suffer.

Learning to be wise is to choose
A life free from suffering.

Contents

A Few Words from the Author About This Book

The *Seeker's Guide to Self-Freedom* is exactly that: an encouraging book in which you will find friendly, helpful guidance and instructions about the new and exciting inner work it takes to wake up and realize your secret True Self. Go beyond the barriers created by the unseen limitations of thought and set yourself free! Here are the keys to a new kind of consciousness that never sabotages itself and that always knows the right thing to do in every moment.

Each chapter is filled with dozens of spiritually empowering insights and special techniques to move you closer and closer to the higher happiness you've been longing for. Helpful question-and-answer sessions reveal powerful methods for dismissing dark emotions and enlarging your relationship with ever-higher states of yourself.

At the close of each chapter are special spiritual exercises. These powerful practices are designed to turn that chapter's lessons in truth into the realization of the truth of those lessons. Each unique spiritual exercise helps you to turn the mere promise of freedom into its fulfillment. You will also discover timeless, yet truly new ways to use all of your relationshiops that will not only help you grow wiser and more compassionate, but that will empower everyone around you to enjoy the same spiritual opportunity.

The *Seeker's Guide to Self-Freedom* shows you how, by being true to your Self, it is possible to conquer the entire world. It is filled with encouraging facts about the path to Real Life and how you can discover the Way for yourself, freeing you from dependency upon any other group or personality. Throughout this book, you will recognize its hundreds of healing truths as your long-lost friends—which they are! And in your growing remembrance of them, they will help you to awaken and remember who you really are.

Introduction

It can be safely said that great are those writings which most clearly reflect reality—that give us insight into life around us by displaying the subtleties of ourselves, showing us all that is wise and noble, dark or deceptive, unique and resourceful. We are each enlarged by these reports, for in them we find ourselves either rediscovered or newly revealed. Writings that can so touch us are rare. But there is another kind of prose; an altogether different order of writing that goes well beyond reflecting our reality to actually *changing* it. Works such as these are known by their ability to undo us; their content mandates a complete reorganization of self not subject to what we have been, but by what we are given to see about ourselves in the truth they reveal.

Writings such as these do more than just temporarily enhance our personal sense of self. They actually stir into us living elements—ideas that are first felt as a breath into us and then begin to breathe for us—bringing back to life the unspeakable memory that our problems have no other source than self-forgetfulness. Through them we begin to live again, but now knowing life as though for the first time. And in the course of their gradual interior leavening, we find at last the meaning of our known universe torn asunder, so that out pours one newly expanded and we riders on its timeless, joyous journey.

I invite you to travel with me on such a journey. We will go past all positive imaginings and, ultimately, beyond the influence of fear itself . . . and when we at last arrive at our destination, we will find ourselves *free*. Why? Because we journey into ourselves. We return to our forgotten heritage and Home within the land of Truth.

The small, handsome sign over the new shop in town was simple. Its handcarved woodblock letters read: Rare Wine Shop. Hanging directly beneath it was a smaller, arrow-shaped sign pointing directly to the always-open shop door. Brightly painted letters spelled out the invitation:

Visitors welcome! Taste the difference!

And inside the shop the lights were always on, so that no one passing by might mistake it for being closed.

One day a young man walked into the store and, after politely greeting the elderly shopowner, asked if he might taste a few of the wines for sale. To his surprise, the owner told him that the store only sold one wine—a rare wine—and of this the shopkeeper would gladly pour him a glass to sample.

Finding it difficult to keep his thoughts to himself in the awkward moments of waiting for the owner to pour the wine, the young man decided to speak his mind: "Isn't it awfully difficult to stay in business selling only *one* kind of wine?"

He didn't know what to make of the shopkeeper's reply, even though it was given with a smile: "I guess it all depends on the nature of one's business." With this the young man was handed a taster's glass of a dark red, richly fragrant wine. The owner kept speaking.

"This wine is not to everyone's taste,"—but there was no apology in his voice. "However," his tone shifting as though trying to convey some unspoken secret, "there are those who, having once tasted this wine, can never again be satisfied with any other."

"We'll have to see," said the young man while lifting the glass to his lips, "*that* would have to be some special wine." Then, doing his best to look cultured enough to know the difference, he sniffed the wine, swirled it around a time or two, and took a deliberately slow, measured sip.

The trembling began in his mouth . . . almost a quiver . . . and it spread to a delicious, almost familiar, warmth, washing over and within him, like being immersed in liquid sunlight. He forgot that he was standing there—even that there was wine in his mouth. So captured by a surge of sensations was he, and equally unable to resist them, that his principle awareness was on how much he hoped the wine shop owner couldn't see what he was experiencing. He noticed that the elder had mercifully turned his back on him to return the wine bottle to the shelf. Quickly he set his sample glass back down on the counter and, composing the most sincere smile he could to cover his strange reaction to the wine, he thanked the shopowner for his hospitality and walked abruptly out the door.

That same evening the young man attended a party given by his closest friends in honor of himself, to celebrate recent good fortune that had come his way. But the afternoon's wine-tasting event remained with him. He felt removed—almost a stranger amongst his own. And even more peculiar was how the wine served that night, which had always been his favorite, tasted so old and lifeless. He drank it nevertheless, glass after glass of it. However, it wasn't for the pleasure of the wine, or to better mingle with his admiring company; he drank to make the night pass quickly, to make his heart forget the way it had been stirred only hours earlier in an obscure wine shop no one else even knew existed. But the more he drank, the more it made him remember.

The next morning, awakening from a fitful sleep, he wasn't at all sure how he got home and into bed. However, there was one thing he was sure about: He wanted, above all else, to put the strange events of the day just past behind him. But this wish wasn't to be.

All he could think about at work, all day long, was that most unusual wine he had sipped the day before. Finally, in a cross between fearing he might be losing his mind and realizing he was unable to do any real work in his current condition, he closed his business for the day and headed straight for the one-wine Rare Wine Shop.

On the way there his thoughts tormented him with mental pictures that the specialty shop would be closed, or worse, perhaps gone out of business. The nearer he drew to the store's location, the greater grew his fear. After all, what would happen to him if he were unable to satisfy this new love of his for the rare wine? So, when the troubled young man arrived at the shop door, he was heartened to see it open. He walked inside, drawing a deep breath as though trying to drink in the whole aromatic atmosphere at once.

The old shopowner looked him over closely, but remained silent. Neither of them spoke, yet much was exchanged in those few first moments. Then the young man, sensing clearly there was no sense in pretending anything, began pleading with the shop owner.

"Please!" he implored, looking down at the rough, wood-planked floor. "You must tell me what's going on here! In less than twenty-four hours since I came here and tasted your wine, I feel as though everything I've ever cared about is as nothing. What's happening to me? All I can think about . . ." (he struggled not to say what he knew he was about to hear himself say) "is this . . . wine!"

His eyes rose to meet the old man's, and in that instant of contact he felt like a small child being evaluated—for something beyond his reasoning—by a caring but obviously detached adult. But what shocked him most was that, clearly, this wine shop owner wasn't the least bit surprised at either his pleading questions or his shaky behavior. And that's when the young man realized he'd asked the old man the wrong question. It shouldn't have been, "What have you done to me?" No! Now he could see that he should have asked, "Who are you?" And finally, confounding him all the more, the very next moment he was listening to the answer to this, his unspoken question:

"Many, many long years ago, in the far country of my homeland, there came a Great War. Nothing like it had ever occurred before . . . or since," the old man added as a kind of afterthought. "Because of the great dangers threatening to overshadow his realm, our great King—long may he reign—decided that the wisest way to protect the scores upon scores of his noble citizens was to send them away to live in certain far points of the nation. There, it was reasoned, they would be safe, be able to thrive, and remain well until the uprising and conflict had passed. Then all could return home." He paused again, thinking over what he had just said. Deciding he had the facts straight, he confirmed, "At least, as I understand it, this was to be the plan."

The elder paused to pour himself a glass of wine and, nodding toward a second glass sitting on the counter, asked if his visitor would enjoy some too. "Please," the young man answered with an enthusiastic nod of his own.

"Anyway," the shopkeeper continued as he poured, "for so long did so many of these men and women live in distant parts of the realm that they, and their children, and their children's children, came to forget all about the country of their origin . . . and, of course, their great King. And that's why I am here in your city. I've been sent to search out these lost citizens and, if they wish, to bring them back to the highlands of their rightful homeland." He lifted up his glass of wine in salute, and the young man did likewise, although he was unsure of just exactly what it was that was being toasted. They both took a full swallow of the wine, savoring both the warmth of it and the moment of their obviously shared enjoyment. The moment lingered. But, at least for one of them, there remained unanswered questions, so the moment wasn't enough.

"Sir, it goes without saying that I'm sorry to hear of anyone losing his or her way in this world, but what does your story have to do with this strange effect that your wine has on me?" He was already beginning to feel the delicious effects of the mouthful he'd swallowed only seconds before, so he wasn't sure if the shopkeeper had only just become more serious or if he had always spoken in that tone now being directed toward him.

"The one wine I sell in my shop is made from certain rare grapes and unique spices growing only in the rich, fertile highland valleys of my beloved country. And while it's true that I do go looking all over the world for those good citizens whose true heritage is our highlands," and again he raised his glass in a silent toast, "*it is this wine that does the finding* . . . for any man or woman, regardless of how long they have been separated from our beloved kingdom, *knows* its flavor. In fact, it's my experience that entire generations may have passed, and their children may have never before tasted this wine in their lifetime, still all it takes is one small sip and they make themselves known to me . . . *just as you have.*"

He paused just long enough to ensure the young man had time to grasp the full meaning of his words. "You see, this wine has the power to stir and to awaken in our people a certain long-slumbering memory. It causes them to recall the place of their true origin. And, once having been awakened this way, *nothing* else really matters to them, other than making their way back to their highland Home." And he smiled at his equally beaming visitor, "Yes . . . all it takes is just one taste."

And again the young man nodded in agreement, only this time, he knew why.

Truths for Living

one

Inviting What Is True to Set You Free

We have all heard, in some way or another, the beautiful, hope-filled words "Know the truth and the truth will set you free."

For millions of people the world over, this idea is connected to a particular religious sentiment that comforts them in times of plenty, but serves little use when these same people find themselves captives of some stress or sorrow produced by an unwanted moment. During these difficult times, the general perception goes something like this: "The *truth* is that life must surely be against me, because if this 'reality of life' weren't looming over me, lurking in the shape of this present shadow, I wouldn't be as afraid or worried as I am now."

So which is it? Does the Truth serve to free us, or do we have to serve painful truths and struggle with them to escape their wrath? Let any uncertainty we have be quietly washed away in the following revelation and explanation—here is the one great truth behind all of our individual experiences, after which we will prove its timeless existence:

The nature of Truth is victory. It is the eternal expression of David and Goliath. Its one great purpose is to empower, free, and fulfill whomsoever should realize it. Now let's see how this is true. We begin with the insights of the great mathematician and sage, Albert Einstein:

> A human being is part of the whole, called by us "Universe"; a part limited in time and space. He experiences himself, his thoughts, his feelings, as something separated from the rest—a kind of optical delusion of his consciousness. This delusion is a kind of prison for us, restricting us to our personal desires and to affection for a few persons nearest to us. Our task must be to free ourselves from this prison by widening our circle of compassion to embrace all living creatures, and the whole of nature in its beauty.

Such holistic sentiments almost always ring true to those with "ears to hear"; yet again we must recognize in the above statement a similar challenge as we do with trying to reconcile the idea that the Truth sets us free. As we all know too well, it's one thing to *want* to be truly free, to be wholly compassionate, and it's another level of consciousness altogether to *know* the Truth that lifts us above the presently small circle of our often-stressed lives. So, the first truth we must realize is that the truths we claim as being ours don't really belong to us; we must admit that something stands between us and the truth that would free us and enlarge our hearts.

Freedom and compassion cannot dwell in any world dominated by fear. And, just for the record, our usual reaction to any event not of our choosing is to fear it, so that our tendency is to see these experiences as being adversarial. These unwanted moments are seen as threats to our present happiness, as well as being thorns in our tomorrow, because with any unwanted event comes the fear of not having the right answers to address the flood of new questions arising out of life's sudden turn.

But what if what we *think* is the truth of these moments is not the truth at all? What if it were possible to see the truth of these moments in a whole new light? Imagine if we could know in any of these given moments that life isn't handing us a bunch of do-or-die questions upon which hinge happiness or defeat—that our unwanted experiences don't deliver us into our enemy's hands, but lead us instead to living answers whose soul purpose is to help us realize the great Friend we have in Truth? Wouldn't such a reality, once realized, end those nagging fears that ride the dark tailcoat of the unexpected? And wouldn't the end of these fears be the same as being free to live fearlessly? Of course! And, as we are about to find out, this is precisely the case.

When we recall the turning points in our lives, the times where we had no choice but to go through those wrenching self-changes that come with personal crisis, it shouldn't be hard to remember how sure we were that these same trials heralded our doom. But looking back, as I invite you to do now, can't we see that the real crisis we faced was one born not so much of changing external conditions as it was of our being asked to take part in the birth of a new level of our own consciousness? A brief consideration proves this crucial, truth-filled finding.

Experience reveals that the actual nature of any painful moment in life has little to do with what we first blame our pain on. For example, that "She wants to leave me" isn't the real pain; the real pain is that if she does, it means there has to be something "wrong" with me. Besides, without her in my life as she has been, I won't know what to do with myself; I'll be uncertain as to the worth of who I am, or how I should view myself. And so, being in fear of having to deal with what feels akin to the end of ourselves, we resist or deny anything that threatens us with such an untimely demise. At this stage, our general response is to make unwanted compromises with ourselves, or otherwise somehow grovel to keep the passing relationship alive. However, try as we might, what will come to pass does just that. Maybe it takes years, months, or maybe only days, but we are slowly dragged through the doorway of a life lesson that is no longer avoidable. And what do we invariably find?

Behind each of these seemingly impossible moments stands an unseen (at the time) purpose: to bring us to a certain realization or experience of the truth about our self. But while this medicine may be bitter, it also heals us. How?

For starters, we realize (in hindsight) that what has transpired was not only a gift in disguise, but that we are much better off for having worked our way through its challenging wrapping! Now we understand, beyond the shadow of any doubt, that we couldn't begin the next level of our life journey until we had completed these lessons now behind us. In other words, it's clear to us that what we first fought so hard to avoid was really a truth come to rescue us from self-ignorance—a truth that not only explained why our lives were as they were, thus freeing us from a mistaken sense of self, but in the same moment set the stage for our further self-development. Can you see the truth of this recurring set of conditions and how it continually manifests itself through the course of our life experiences? We have reached the threshold of the Great Truth.

We have realized that our experiences in life ultimately serve the purpose of revealing some unseen truth about us, to us. As this is the truth, amply evidenced by our own accounting, then can we not begin to perceive that these very experiences, regardless of their content, must be an expression of the truth for the purpose of helping us discover the truth behind these same life experiences? To help you more deeply understand this liberating insight, let's view it from a slightly different angle.

Each cycle of our life, as marked by each subsequent level of personal growth, comes to a happy close only when the lessons driving that cycle are finally learned. This much should be clear to us. But what remains cloudy is that each life lesson learned that served to close out each cycle came to us in the form of a needed truth. And further, that this same truth always arrives in some distinct realization about our own nature—one that had not only been unconscious to us, but that is now recognized as having been secretly responsible for the events of that life cycle now being exited. Can you see the tremendous implications in this finding?

First, it means that in the middle of any unwanted experience, waiting there all along for us to realize it, is the truth that liberates and lifts us above our former limited understanding responsible for that very experience. In other words, our experiences revolve around, and are actually created to reveal, certain life lessons yet to be learned. And if we would dare see further (which we must if we would know Truth's victory), this discovery reveals the unimaginable. There exists behind these life lessons a timeless truth, one that has not only perceived what we need *before* we do, but that somehow actively arranges our life experiences for the sole purpose of revealing itself to our soul.

We have set before us evidence of a completely compassionate, purposeful Intelligence—a living Truth whose silent operation not only reveals the meaning of our existence but serves in this capacity as seed, nourishment, and fruition of our incredibly diverse life-experiences. To grasp, even in the smallest way, that a wisdom revealed to us as Truth (call it what you will) is the secret fabric of our lives, is to begin realizing a whole new order of self-victory. Here we come upon a success that has no opposite. Failure ceases to exist as a fear. The painful idea of loss, of falling down and losing our way, forever loses its sting, because in the light of our new understanding we see now that the universe itself not only wants us to be victorious individuals, but actually wills this special victory.

Expanding Our Understanding of the Nature of Truth

It seems that everywhere I go today, everyone has their own idea of what the truth is and why I should support their idea or value system. So my question is, what is truth and how do I come upon it for myself?

Start simply. It may not seem so at the outset of your journey, but the Truth is always simple. For instance, here is a simple truth to ponder: Thought tends to confuse what is true; it twists it. No one has to tell us this truth. We can see it anytime we go into denial or self-justification. Here the mind races to resolve its own contradictions. For instance, when it finally yields to the truth that of itself it cannot succeed at rescuing itself, in the same moment we see two truths: First, how thought confuses the truth, and second, how evident the truth of this is on the other side of the storm . . . all of which reveals another truth: Truth is self-evident. And so we come upon the one truth that is the gateway to the Truth we seek: Know thyself. Can you see the beauty in this root truth? No one else need be depended upon for the way to the Truth that sets us free, for it resides right within us. What this means to us is that we need no other authority in our lives beyond those truths we are willing to learn about ourselves.

Is the idea that the truth knows "all is well" simply a matter of faith, or are there facts to support it?

There are facts supporting the Truth's statement that all is well, but it takes "eyes that can see" them. We live in a perfectly ordered universe, a system of infallible balance. To be able to see this invisible world, with all of its perfect workings, ensures for anyone who can see it that not only is all well, but that there is no essential need for fear. The more we are able to inwardly perceive this orderly universe, the greater our ability is to let go of ourselves and allow the Intelligence that created this order to do what it has been secretly doing all along, which is to invite us to take part in it. Our work is about seeing the truth of all this and allowing our discoveries to guide us to the higher destination of which they hint.

I have read the words of certain saints and masters, all of whom allude to the idea that the stars line up for those who seek the Celestial. If this is true (and I hope it is!), why does truth want us to succeed in realizing its promise for us?

If you can see the validity of the following idea as it operates in your everyday life, you will see the Celestial truth behind it: Haven't you ever loved someone, and out of this love wanted more for them than they even knew to imagine? So it is with Truth's wish, with the Creator's wish for us.

So many ideas abound today about the nature of truth. I don't know what to believe, especially with all this business about "creating your own reality." Is truth simply subjective to each individual? In other words, is there only truth according to each person?

Firstly, if we are awake, we can learn to see "the Celestial in the common" all around us, that in all things this scale of life promises a true and incorruptible beginning. What this source is called has no bearing on its reality and its ability to act as a beacon for those who are tired of walking around in the dark. Secondly, beliefs are not the issue; the issue is the nature that holds them, which is why we must come to an understanding of levels of being and of scale. Absolutely there is an Absolute Truth. But the fact of *this* Truth does not negate the fact that we are lost and struggling on this planet only because presently we are each, to whatever degree, living out the effects of a subjective truth and the "reality" it produces. This subjective reality is the illusion, the dream from which we are to awaken. When this dream ends, so does the dreaming self. The truth of an awakened life is the same for all so aware.

How can we recognize and authenticate universal spiritual truths?

How does an eagle know an eagle? Or a lion another lion? As you awaken inwardly, there will be an instantaneous and growing recognition of what is true. There will be no mistaking this understanding.

Would you please explain what is meant by "karma"? There must be more to it than just the simplistic notion that we get back what we do!

You're right. Better stated is that we get back from life what *we are*. This is the truth of our reality, and though it may not appear to be so, we live in a universe that is an absolutely perfectly balanced system. Every request we make of life produces a response. To this truth there are no exceptions. As we learn that our attention, whether seen or not, animates what it is directed upon (thoughts, etc.), we come to understand that even unconscious thoughts or actions are indeed a request. These requests are always answered. That is karma, and this is perfect justice.

I strongly sense that in order to see deeper into my own inner life, I need to understand that timeless truth, "As above, so below." Yet, when I try to think this truth through in order to understand it, everything gets hazy. Would you please explain the idea of things being in "scale"?

The understanding of scale begins with seeing the world we live in as a microcosm of macrocosmic life. For example, in the veins of a leaf or even in the Mississippi Delta, we can see the form and image of our own circulatory system. Or take the form and action of a simple atom. Within it we can see the shape and action of our solar system. New ideas such as these, which help us to see the world around us in new and broader ways, help develop this important form of higher understanding. But its power for healing, and ultimately freeing us from ourselves, is based not so much in "knowledge" of this scale as it is through being in touch with its truth through our own higher emotional parts. Spend time by yourself outdoors. Look at trees. Lose yourself in a starry night sky. Feel sunlight pulsing on your skin while you notice the beat of your own heart. Give yourself a chance to embrace all of what you see. In these common expressions of life that we will enter into in this way, a secret window is found through which we can see a reflection of a larger, Celestial Life. Your wish to understand this larger Life (of which you are already a part) arises from a part of you that will, in time, reveal itself to you.

One truth I've struggled with is the notion that "there is nothing new under the sun." Would you please explain this highly esoteric idea that everything that ever was or ever will be already exists?

Our perception of time is based upon both the natural operation of the senses, which register life as originating outside of ourselves, and through thought, whose nature it is to perceive all things through opposites. This physically centered self "knows" itself through the sensations these characteristics produce, i.e., passing time. But there is another level of development that stands inwardly in relationship to a whole other order of self. Although this higher self registers physical movement and recognizes the existence of created time, it dwells nevertheless in a world that, like itself, is unchanging. From this vantage point, it is understood that all that exists, and ever did or will, has always been. And, incidentally, real freedom begins with this stage of self-knowledge.

New Knowledge About Our True Nature

I have read in a number of sources that we are not living from our own will but from a "false will." If this false will is not what we are intended to express, why is it so strong and natural-feeling, while working *not* to express it seems unnatural?

All inner conditions, mental and emotional (even chemical), constantly strive for homeostasis, or a balance among themselves determined by themselves. We are "made," created to live from and within the parameters of these internal conditions—even the worst, most destructive ones, such as substance addictions. So, in a manner of speaking, it is "natural" for us to feel the resistance these states throw at us when we attempt to step outside of their content. This explains the importance of self-studies and the higher reason that is born through self-discovery. We must learn to do what we know is true about our condition (whatever that condition may be, or whatever it may be telling us) instead of allowing that condition to tell us what is true about ourselves. This is the only way in which we will come to find that our True Nature is unconditional.

I don't really understand why so many spiritual paths teach that we are not our thoughts and feelings. If we are not these things, then what exactly are we?

I know that this idea seems confusing at first. Nevertheless, it is true: You are not your thoughts and feelings any more than you are your hands (alone) holding up this book for your eyes to read and mind to grasp. Thoughts and feelings (as with your physical body) are aspects of yourself. To be asleep spiritually is to be fully identified with these thoughts and feelings that call themselves you. To awaken is to begin realizing the truth of this and to savor the new relationship within you that this realization grants.

Could you clarify what is meant in the spiritual idea that we don't so much breathe as we are ourselves breathed?

If all of us were to come wide awake, right now, we would realize that our hearts are beating, our lungs are taking air in and out, and all of it occurs with virtually no awareness of these functions on our part. To experience the fact that there is a Real Heart behind (and within) the drum that beats in you begins with learning to be awake to even these elementary lessons in physical awareness. Our lives are indeed given to us. At all levels Life lives through us, moment to moment.

Can you help shed some light on why we are here in this life?

All of our deeper personal experiences eventually come to reveal some lesson that we needed to learn. This process of events that leads us to the discovery of their cause proves both the existence of order and purpose. The outcome of each experience turns out to be for personal growth. Therefore, it is safe to say we are here on earth, in these bodies, to grow in wisdom and the love that is an outgrowth of it.

How in the world did we get here? Did we first have to progress to a certain level before we could be admitted passage to this earth? I keep trying to figure out what I must have done wrong!

Questions such as this one have no bearing on our inner work to be free. All such speculative thinking belongs, in general, to our imagining parts—aspects of self that are more comfortable dealing with what isn't than going into what is. We must all learn this difference. Real spiritual work is not about what may be—but about being willing to fully engage this life of ours as it *is*. In these facts, and these alone, are we given all that we need to know about all possible worlds.

I have often read that our True Nature is part of a timeless life and was wondering if you could tell me something about this possibility. Everything I do and feel is based upon redeeming some past blunders or grasping for a brighter future.

The timeless life can never really be defined, only realized in varying degrees depending upon the individual's receptivity, but let's consider just a few characteristics of this True Nature as an awakened person might experience them. They include an abiding sense of the Eternal, which is never apart from one's own self; the direct knowledge that "you" are somehow situated in the center of the universe and, as such, that everything in life is not only created just for you, but waits for you to claim it; and certainly not last, and by no means least, a deep awareness of participating in a great purpose and plan to life, coupled with an unshakable confidence that nothing can interfere with its success.

Five Truths That Make You Victorious

The potential height of any truthful principle, with its commanding view of life, remains essentially groundless for us unless we agree to reach above ourselves and enter into the realm of its superior reality. In other words, and to bring us to the point of the special exercises that follow, Truth can only convey its liberating powers upon us to the degree that we are willing to explore the freedom it promises.

When those familiar feelings wash over us that we have somehow failed at something, or that we are sure to face defeat should we endeavor to claim some personal higher ground, we can do much better than allow ourselves to be carried away by these dark waves. We can call upon the following five light-filled truths to realize new self-victory. Study these friendly facts until they tell you why the whole idea of failure, including the painful sense of self it creates, is a lie you need no longer live with.

Truth #1

The truth is . . . nothing in life can stop you from starting your life all over, at any time, because the true fabric of life is a cosmic weave of ceaseless beginnings. That's right. Your power for starting over is backed up by Reality itself, which will place its supreme strength on the side of whoever chooses it over self-ruinous states. All that is needed to put the power of this ever-renewing truth to work in your life is for you to consciously agree to view any unwanted or unhappy moment *not* as some unavoidable ending, but as the temporary and passing condition that it really is.

Truth #2

The truth is . . . just as our own physical eye can't see itself other than by gazing upon a reflection of itself, we can't see our psychological self other than by gazing upon those mental images of our own creation. So, when "seeing" a failure in our mind's eye, we need only remember in that very moment this truth: It is we ourselves who put it there! Now, instead of feeling defeated by how we picture ourselves, we can see through this defeated feeling itself by daring to see all the way back to how this painful painting came into existence in the first place.

Truth #3

The truth is . . . that just as it is impossible to feel ourselves a "failure" without having first condemned ourselves for some shortcoming, to do so tells of a secret self-duality that is the seed of defeat. Study the following truth closely: In order to see ourselves as being "small," we must be standing over ourselves *at the same time*. Now see that neither of these selves within us can exist in our mind's eye without the other, and that being self-divided like this, we must feel as though we are going to topple over and fall. But seeing the truth that we are neither of these interdependent selves unites us in a higher understanding that is fail-safe.

Truth #4

The truth is . . . the painful identity that results from thinking of yourself as a failure can exist only for as long as you cling to some self-created, self-sinking label. The only reason you won't abandon this sinking ship of yourself is because in its cargo hold is stored all your cherished ideas about what it means to be a success. The discovery of this truth reveals that the only weight dragging you under is your best ideas about how to sail through life.

Truth #5

The truth is . . . even the most superficial glance at the world in which we live shows us, beyond any doubts, that there is nothing living that is not a work in progress. This encouraging fact of life reveals a great secret from which we can draw true comfort in times of our trials. Even when it feels like life might just break us, these same trying moments are only part of the Truth's broader plan to *make* us stronger, wiser, and more willing to delve into the truth of our existence.

two

Steps to Possessing Your True Self

Have you ever thrown your hands in the air and asked yourself "What in the world is going on with me? How come my best intentions and the ability to accomplish them seem to live in two different universes?"

We intend *not* to run off like a mad human being, spending money ill-afforded. We intend *not* to do something mean-spirited or otherwise self-defeating. Yet that is often just what we do. Then we ask, "What happened . . . how could we?" Yet, for all of our questioning, this mystery remains unsolved. To paraphrase St. Paul, we don't do what we know is right, and do instead what we sense is all wrong for us.

Part of the answer to this endless enigma requires an understanding of its own hidden dynamic—knowledge hard come upon because the self that continually runs into these problems is itself a part of the problem that it faces. With this idea in mind, see if the following insight doesn't shed much-needed light into this darkness of our spiritual inability.

No intention can be any stronger than our ability to remember it in the moment that it is needed. Considering this fact brings us to a vital discovery about our present nature.

The reason we can't remember our intention is because we are not *one* self. We are a being fragmented into many parts, all of which have separate agendas and therefore individual intentions.

As you have no doubt witnessed, these various aspects of self "argue" with one another—one tugging this way, the other that way—and all are unconscious of the fact that their conflict consumes our life's energy. In effect, our time is spent trying to be accountable by pleasing one master after another within ourselves—only there is no pleasing this "self" (or any other, as they pop up in this psychological chain of false command).

However, when you can see how one part of yourself manages to take control of the rest of you, it is the beginning of the end of its authority over you. To state this same idea in other words, this new and higher form of self-discernment begins with realizing that you are in wrong relationship with these false parts of yourself—that you are not intended to be their servant, but the other way around! Within this discovery begins the process of letting go of the anxiety and worry that must attend being unconsciously identified with these temporary characters within yourself.

As you realize that your greater intentions are rendered powerless in the hands of these vagrant parts of yourself, it also becomes evident that you are not going to be able to fulfill these higher aims until you begin to become a whole human being. But how can self-unification take place when this aim itself is thwarted at every turn by the very nature it seeks to replace? This question brings us to the solution of a great spiritual mystery.

The more we awaken to how inwardly divided we actually are—and start to see all of the forces randomly operating within us, with no guidance apart from the "good" each separate self desires at the moment—the more we realize the need for a new kind of unity, a wholeness we are unable to create by ourselves, within ourselves.

With this new understanding comes the dawning that the only way to accomplish our higher intentions in life is to start embracing God's intention for us to be whole and conscious creatures. Our will must be redirected, married to a Greater One.

In this gradual redirection of our "willingness," a new sense of self begins to surface in us; no longer do we struggle to will ourselves into being strong or righteous; no more do we turn on ourselves for our "weakness."

These former choices, once thought of as being part of what we needed to succeed with our intention, are now recognized as being part of the problem and not the solution. Our new intention is simply to remember God in our life, and this will becomes the one part of ourselves with which we meet everything that life brings to us.

Suffering (for whatever reasons) ceases to be our focus; nor is what might happen to us tomorrow of any more concern. The issue in moments of trial (or victory) becomes simply remembering where our heart is supposed to be. And within this new way of knowing ourselves rests the active understanding that anything in us that doesn't embrace this higher willingness is secretly set against our new and truer intention . . . which brings us to one last consideration.

Nature abhors a straight line. And what the unaided eye sees everywhere, the sciences confirm. By law, substances tend to circle themselves. What this means to anyone seeking the way out is that the spiritually sleeping person doesn't know that he or she is simply going 'round and 'round, caught in the unconscious circle of self whose secret intention is the re-creation of itself.

This is why a new and higher understanding of our internal workings is so necessary. "Know thyself" takes on the meaning once lost (and now forgotten) as the only way of possessing ourselves. Without this self-understanding, we remain captives of a level of consciousness that believes going in circles leads somewhere. It doesn't.

Freedom from the False Self

I have read in various writings (including your own) the description of many selves that seem to dwell within us at our unseen expense. You have called this nature the "Temporary Person in Charge." There are so many times I wish I could just be rid of these temporary selves, but nothing I do seems to give me the self-control I seek. What can I do?

Sufi teachings speak of the "commanding self," Christianity of deceitful interior "friends," and virtually all other religions hold forth the idea that we have many "I's" or divergent personalities within us, and also that some of these selves are for us and some against us. My term "Temporary Person in Charge" describes the appearance of various yet familiar I's that appear within us to respond to the ever-changing flow of life. Key to grasp here is that each newly surfacing "I" we take as being our true self isn't conscious to us until some problem presents itself. With our once-shaky sense of "I" vested in this new and commanding "I" (that knows what needs to be done to put life aright), we again feel in control of our lives. What remains unseen by us is that each of these false I's is, in reality, a kind of shadow self—its actual nature little more than a temporary substructure of thought fashioned from the content of our own past experience. What this means is that this "self"—which seems to solve our problems—is, in fact, a part of the problems' recurring appearance. Think about this deeply: The self that resists any other self is itself an extension of the self it is resisting. This is why we must stay awake and work to remain in the present moment. If we can remain observant to the appearance and running around of these vagrant

I's—as opposed to identifying with one of them—we can be free of their limiting influences.

What exactly should you do or try to understand when you first catch one of these false selves trying to drag you into its life?

If someone walked into your room right now and started firing off instructions, particularly ones you recognized as being self-defeating in nature, would you have any trouble knowing how to handle such a person or his orders? When we can see psychic intruders clearly as being the uninvited internal intrusion that they are, our inner response is immediate and effective. We go silent. Our silence is their walking papers. If, however, the visitor-in-thought doesn't leave, but becomes more insistent, all the better ground upon which you stand to recognize this entity as a foe, not a friend. As a good guideline, remember: Our thoughts are intended to serve us, not steal from us. Make the distinction clearer inwardly and your inner actions will be amplified according to that clarity. There is something within each of us that knows the difference between what is good for us and what isn't.

I believe I am becoming aware of the false self more and more consistently. How many times do I have to come awake to its trickery before I can be free of it?

Think about what you are asking here. I'll paraphrase your question for you as your answer: "How many times a day do I have to keep myself from falling into a hole? How many times a day must I invest myself in something that can never be taken away from me?" Add to these ideas one more insight and invitation for further self-study: The unattended mind is a breeding ground for self-defeat.

> At times I am able to see certain places in myself where I am painfully identified or attached to external objects or internal thoughts and feelings. But for the life of me I can't get clear in my head what "identifying" is. I seem to think I know, but every time I attempt to put my thoughts on paper, I get lost.

First let me encourage you to continue the work of making your own mind clear on this (or any) spiritual subject by getting down on paper what you understand about it. There is tremendous benefit in this practice. As far as being identified: It is an unconscious process that occurs when our thoughts, having formed an image of someone or something, then embrace this image as the thing itself they have imagined. We unknowingly derive a sense of "I" from each mental or emotional image thus inwardly considered, and it is this sense of self that sits at the root of attachment—the "punishment of being identified." Understanding this inner dynamic helps us see why letting go is so difficult, because it is never the thing, but our own prized sense of self, that must be released.

> Can you help me understand why I give myself away so often? I know I do it, but I am never aware of this self-defeating behavior *while* I'm doing it.

Have you ever asked yourself, "What in the world did I just do?" or "Why did I say that cruel thing?" Who are you talking to? If *you* didn't sink your own ship, then who did? Something took you over. The beauty of staying awake within ourselves and remaining watchful and aware is that it is possible to see the truth of this and to be in relationship with that which never gives itself away to any negative condition. This means that when we do give ourselves away, each time we compromise ourselves without knowing it, we are asleep in that moment to what we are in relationship with. Awakening is about ending our unconscious relationship with that level of our present nature that not only gives itself away hand over fist, but also is always looking for new and better ways to do it!

There are times when truthful ideas make perfect sense and really hit home. At other times, something in me just rebels at higher ideas. I know that this part of me is my false nature, but could you tell me more about why it rears its ugly head in this way?

An important part of our work to awaken to the Truth that frees us begins with awakening to those selves in us that are actually set against us realizing Real Life. Make no mistake: These insidious I's do not want you in the light, because the darkness that drives them can neither enter nor live there.

Is repeating a mantra or employing other spiritual disciplines helpful in our efforts to get out of the circle of self?

Escaping the circle of self depends entirely upon understanding its nature. If we use mantras, or give ourselves to any other discipline whose purpose is to somehow empower us to escape the prison of our sleeping self, then in this order of action we merely empower this same captivating nature we wish to be free from. Our intent must be moment-to-moment, right now, *to be present* to ourselves. When this is our intention, then practicing prayer, or mantras, or whatever, becomes valuable—because it serves and nourishes our wish to be free, instead of leading us to mistake these practices for freedom itself.

Start Discerning and Living from Your True Self

How can we know when what we are experiencing is from the Truth and not from our fabricated self?

How do we know the difference between a lemon and a peach? Between an organic apple and a waxed look-alike? Keep working and you will acquire a greater and greater ability to "taste" your own inner states. Then you will know the difference between self-provided experiences of one order and those provided for you by and in a higher context.

What is it that I call gut instinct that lets me know what the real answers are to things without even going into thought? I seem to "know" answers, even if people lie to me, trying to cover up what I sense is true.

What you speak of is a form of intuition, i.e., the innate ability to sense the truth of various moments. This gift comes to us from a higher part of one of our centers able to instantly qualify characteristics because it doesn't think toward them, but actually enters into relationship with them. In this relationship it knows what it embraces, thereby knowing the truth (or not) of their expression. This capability of ours explains why the more truth we have in our lives, the safer we are in all situations.

I think I have been trying to overcome my present nature instead of working to understand it and let it go. Would you please comment on this trap? What are some indications that we are relying on the wrong part of ourselves to guide us?

Your intuition is right. In the long run, what self-discovery reveals is that there is no separate self apart from relationship. The more awake we can be to the fact of each moment—and the relationships it encompasses—the clearer everything becomes for us. As we grow in this way, we see it's not a question of "transforming" ourselves, but of *agreeing* to be transformed by what we now are able to realize as the ground of our real life. Keep going. Your question indicates you are on the right track!

From my experience, discovering the True Self is very challenging. On the other hand, one can see an instant transformation in individuals who participate in tele-vangelistic-type events. Why does it have to be so much work to make real changes in ourselves?

What you see in almost all of these moments where someone has a "conversion" experience is usually a certain peak emotional moment wherein the person is elevated by a flood of positive feelings about Christ's life, or salvation, etc. What you don't see is that these emotions (all emotions) are in time—which means they pass. And when they do, the beautiful, loving swan of the moment before returns to the ugly duckling. Real transformation can begin with such epiphanous moments, but for the change to be real, through and through, one must die to oneself . . . a task that takes intentionally sustained inner work.

I have realized my memory has created a made-up self, and that if I just watch my mental workings, that I don't give this made-up self any more energy to keep it alive. Am I on the right track just watching all this mental and emotional stuff run its course?

Yes, keep ever-watchful. Two natures really do exist within each of us even though one (lower) resides within the (Higher) other. Here is a rough gauge by which to discern the two: "Lower self" feels itself ever incomplete. It endlessly pursues a sense of completion by reconfiguring itself, using its own content as its matrix. "Higher Self" seeks nothing; it is already complete.

Suppose I acknowledge the fact that I have several I's operating in me. Which "I" do I go with when they all claim to be the right "I"?

Perhaps a little more light will help you in your decision. There are parts of us that want the Truth, and then there are parts of us that only want what allows us to be comfortable and content with our life as we have known it. The upward path requires taking one step after another into what the self that perceives itself as doing this "walking" will feel is precarious, and perhaps even dangerous. But be assured, there is no danger to any human being who puts the Truth before all else, including his or her fear of making a mistake. As best you can, follow the "I" that wants the skies for its Home. This self, although not Real "I," has the wings you need, and will help lift you if you will keep your "I" intent upon its lead.

If God wills everything, what then is free will?

Picture a woman in a bakery shop. She has free will to order and eat anything she likes as long as it is made of bread.

Awaken the New Perception
That Is Pressure-Free

When we turn on a faucet connected to a hose with a small nozzle at its other end, we know from experience that we have to keep the hose in hand, otherwise we will likely get soaked chasing down the runaway end. What happens is that the water pressure, as it passes through the nozzle, transforms our ordinarily tame garden hose into the equivalent of a tethered rocket.

With this picture in mind, can you also see that when we are angry or anxious, the same principle holds true in us, as it does in the hose example, of too much pressure and too little release? Heated thoughts or runaway emotions flood through our psychic system, pick us up, and cause us to career wildly until we crash into whatever unfortunate thing may be in our path.

Now, when it comes to our chores, and the hose runs wild, we can either turn off the water or simply widen the spray of the nozzle and our problem is solved. But when our constricted consciousness reaches critical mass and starts throwing us around, how do we resolve this pressure?

It should be clear by now that our usual approach to venting this pressure provides, at best, only temporary relief. What we really need isn't a Band-Aid, but an inner healing. This need brings us, once again, and yet in still another way, to the time-honored truth of "Know thyself." Only the understanding of our actual inner condition shows us what can free us, otherwise we wind up the servant of our own inner pressure, doing what it bids us to do instead of being its master.

Commanding the pressures of this life begins with understanding that the stress we feel is first an inside job. In and of itself, there is no such thing as a "pressurized" moment. Try to see the truth of this.

The present moment flows along freely. Nothing can possibly restrict what is ever refreshing itself in the ever-new *Now*. This finding reveals that any pressure we come to feel in any given moment is the unhappy effect of some hidden agent within us acting on the ordinarily free-flowing content of each of these moments. In no time at all, the quiet and naturally unrestricted stream of events around us becomes a jet engine within us, rocketing us out of peace.

Now, in our physical world, whenever the garden hose gets "charged" and starts to whip around, we simply realize what has happened, reach down, and turn off the water. But in the spiritual world within us, we can't "turn off" life! It pours itself out in an eternal outflow, which brings us to an important question. If it is not the movement of life itself that restricts us, where then is the hidden bottleneck wrecking our inner world? There can only be one answer to this timeless question, although it may be stated in different ways.

It is our own narrow mind, with its narrow view of life, that pressurizes our events and their moments. This small mind, which can't be separated from the narrow world it perceives, tends to see life's events not as they are, but as what they are *not*, according to its own unconscious demands.

In other words, the punishing pressure we feel in this life is not because of what life is but because of what we perceive life *isn't*—a judgment that could neither be reached nor sustained were it not for there being within us an unseen "board of governors" that had already concluded what "best" serves us and what won't. But see the contradiction in this discovery and you will free yourself of the pressure created in its undetected presence.

Whenever you serve this painful pressure within you, to somehow release yourself from it by doing the dance it prescribes, it is not *your* interests you serve, but the hidden interests of some small self—the one that has been "telling" you all along what your real pleasures are by punishing you when they seem out of reach!

The next time some pressure starts to build within you, learn to use it to shake yourself awake. Rouse yourself to the pure fact that whatever stress you are starting to feel doesn't really belong to *you*. Stand back from yourself long enough to see that pressurized thoughts and feelings can only arise from a narrow view of life that belongs to a narrow self—a false self that you had momentarily and mistakenly taken as your own. Then just quietly drop this formerly unconscious conclusion. This same moment of letting go releases you from this restricted sense of self and the narrow life it creates.

three

Realize the Promise of Yourself in the Present Moment

One sure measure of spiritual growth is found in our developing awareness that each and every present moment of our lives is a special kind of spiritual looking glass. Within its reflection, for those with "eyes to see," are two quite definite and life-altering perceptions.

First, we may see that each unfolding moment of our life—every experience we have—reveals and yields the fruits of our past actions, what we "reap" from life. Secondly, these same revealing experiences of self also serve as the seeds of our experiences to come—all of which depend upon how we use these seeds. In this fashion it can be said that every life moment is a mirror in which we may gaze upon what we have been and what we may become, and witness both in the same instant.

Imagine the powerful, positive potential such a state of self-seeing makes possible for anyone willing to develop such an inner vision. Without stretching thought too much, we can see the possibility of instant self-correction as well as perfect self-direction. For instance, taken even at its simplest level, just being able to perceive and then drop one troubled moment, to detect and reject one punishing thought or feeling, would be the same as ensuring us happier, less troublesome moments to come. And that's just for starters! But before we discuss the benefits of a higher consciousness that can choose its own content and subsequent experiences, we should do just a bit of preparatory groundwork. We need to understand what coming into this higher state of self-awareness requires of us. What does it mean to "be awake"?

To begin with, let's examine the everyday idea of what it means to awaken. In that appointed hour, when it's time to take our rest, we go to bed and off to sleep. Once refreshed, we awaken from our slumber. These two naturally alternating states of self are normally thought of as representing a time for us when, asleep, we are unconscious of the world around us and then, in coming awake, we become conscious of our surroundings and ourselves. True enough. But even sea cucumbers and potato plants go to sleep and wake up. Their cycles of activity and rest—their relative readiness or not—are not too dissimilar from the rotation of our own physical human cycles.

Surely our "self," with whatever elements it shares in common with this Earth's lower-natured creatures, must have within it something of a higher nature than these machines of surf and soil—creatures that must serve nature without choice. And we do possess this greater nature. Within each of us is the potential for a higher, limitless life—a state of being that is to our present nature what it is to the sheep and dog it stands above. This statement is no mere conjecture, nor is it vain hope. It is a fact that must be explored. So, let's do just that.

Hidden within and above us exist many levels, possible degrees of being more and more inwardly awake. Borrowing a phrase of Christ and turning it slightly will help make our point up to now: There are as many stages of being awake in ourselves, to ourselves, as there "are mansions to explore in my Father's Kingdom." Now, before we venture any further, let's gather the proof of these last few ideas by calling upon some self-evident facts.

For purposes of our first example, imagine two sisters on their way to an important business meeting at their own office center just across the park from where they both live. Halfway through their stroll of the park lane that connects their eastside apartments to the westside business section of the city, a flash of some crystal-like lights catches the eye of Beth, the elder of the two sisters. Her attention is drawn just ahead, to the far side of a small lake in the park center. And there, upon its waters, tens of thousands of sunlight diamonds are dancing to the tempo of a morning breeze. As she watches, rapt in the motion of light, two white geese swim slowly and directly into the heart of these diamond-lit waters, and seem to disappear as if dissolved in the shimmering.

Beth draws in a slow, deep breath. A sense of quiet gratitude washes over her heart and she almost feels as if—should she just dare to let go—she too would disappear into the light. But her moment of enchantment is broken by the sound of Marta's voice. Her sister is anxious to resolve their strategy, one more time, for the business merger meeting before them. Turning slowly to look at her face, Beth sees that Marta doesn't see either the lake before them or its magical display of lights. She also realizes, for the moment anyway, that Marta can't see anything other than the high-stakes meeting to come, so she just acknowledges her concerns and they walk on.

Less then thirty minutes later, seated across the negotiating table from the potential buyers of their company, both of them listen to what amounts to a significant offer. Both Beth and Marta listen to their suitor's proposal and promising terms. Both hear the exact same words being spoken but, as events will prove too true in the time to come, Beth hears the sound of a lie in the major tenant of this takeover bid and is decidedly wary. Marta, half-listening, half-envisioning the Colorado mountain ski chalet she will buy with her newly found fortune, hears only what she wants to hear. In the end, after having to argue in private with Marta, Beth's take on the meeting prevails. A special provision is written into the contract that months afterward saves their company from entering into a disastrous relationship.

What is the discernable difference between these two equally successful women? One is present for a priceless show of lights on the waters even as the other feels the pangs of a time yet to even exist. One can hear the false ring in the sound of a voice that promises the world to her and the other hears only her own thoughts pressing her to accept a dream come true, even if it seems "too good."

The answer to this question—of what sets one sister apart from the other, and how they can have such divergent experiences of life under a set of shared circumstances—leads us to the proof of the existence of the Higher Self we all seek. And more, this same answer reveals all we will need to know about how to make contact with this ever-new and limitless nature within ourselves. Here it is:

In life, our experience of ourself is tied directly to what we are awake to in each passing moment. In other words, *we share our consciousness with what we attend to within our mind.* This timeless truth explains why being aware of ourselves, being mindful in the present moment, counts for everything when it comes to the content of our consciousness.

Who among us has not stood somewhere beneath a starlit night sky, gazed upward, and not felt a certain state of timelessness, as though it were the heart of our very own essence? And conversely, who hasn't been crushed by a petty grievance with a friend or loved one and felt the pummeling of our own thoughts, even as we're unable to stop this troubled thinking?

Are you beginning to make the connection that we ourselves are secretly connected to whatever we hold in our heart and mind? That we can (and do) share in the nature of whatever we attend to? And that this power, to be at one with what we inwardly behold, grants us the power to choose what level of life we want to share in and what levels we do not?

Now to these findings add the fact that everything our True Heart longs for already exists. And more, that this contentment and freedom exists *now*—already present in the moment. If we can see the truth of this we can also see the possibility of a whole new way of meeting life. Before us is a new way of living wherein what we are able to receive from each passing moment depends not upon what we want to extract from it, but resides in how fully awake and aware we can be within its unfolding. Which brings us to yet another important truth: It is the awakened life alone that answers our question of how to have a complete, truly free life.

Being awake and aware of ourselves, as fully self-present as possible, brings us closer and closer to the self-wholeness we search for everywhere—everywhere, that is, but in the one place it is ultimately found, within us, within the moment. But, unlike other self-enriching practices such as sharpening our skills in the arts or sciences, being present-minded is not something we learn in conventional ways. To be awakened to itself, the mind must first *know* itself. What, then, can teach this way?

We begin to reach and stand upon the ground of the present moment by gradually awakening to the effects of being in time—of living from thoughts that only distance us from the very contentment they promise. By this I mean we need to awaken increasingly to the painful effects that arise out of knowing ourselves through those parts of ourselves that only examine life without daring to enter it. And as this new self-awareness grows within us, so too it begins to dawn upon us that where we *need* to live is where Life awaits us . . . in the fully present moment.

Wake Up and Put Yourself in the Present Moment

If we live grounded in the present moment at all times, are we still as susceptible to being overcome by negative states?

It is not that negative states are unable to come over us, but when we stay awake, these random, negative forces can find no home in which to linger. There is an old Chinese saying: "The birds of sadness may fly over your head, but who says they have to build a nest there?"

Sometimes when I feel most awake, I have the feeling that I am hovering over my body, looking down on what is happening. Is this a reliable measure of my being truly mindful of the moment?

There is a natural separation, an indefinable sense of detachment, as a person gradually awakens. But for the purpose of clarity, let me stress that being in this world, but not of it, doesn't mean that we are literally "out of it." We must all work to be watchful of where our ever-fruitful imagination may be working overtime. Here is a good rule of thumb: Are you more quietly in charge of yourself or not?

Over the years of my search for spiritual understanding, I have heard the expression that we should learn to "watch and wait." What does this mean?

In the original Aramaic (the language of the New Testament), to "watch and wait" meant to "stay awake." Our lives, and their quality (or absence of it), are determined by what we are in relationship with from moment to moment within ourselves. This is where we have free will—to be able to choose with what we will share our consciousness. Being awake allows us to discern and drop what is antithetical to real life, while learning to wait reveals that all things pass through us when we are watchful.

> Would you please explain what it means to "remember" yourself? I have read about this same idea in the teachings of the Desert Fathers, certain Buddhist texts, as well as in some Fourth Way schools. This idea of remembering myself resonates in me. It seems important to understand and, more importantly, to be able to do.

Yes, you are correct. Here is some help. Working to remember yourself doesn't mean to think about or otherwise consider yourself, as that is all most of us do all the time anyway. Remembering yourself is quite the opposite of this form of self-considering. To remember yourself begins with realizing you have been asleep, taking part in a self-centered life instead of the God-centered one. You may think of the idea of remembering yourself as simply being aware that "you" are both house and its contents, and that if this house (or awareness of yourself) doesn't know it's there, doesn't know it "stands" in and of itself while the contents rattle around and change position within it, then you are identified totally with the contents . . . which means you are asleep to yourself. Bad dreams are inevitable in this kind of spiritual slumber! To awaken (at least at one important level) is to realize that a house divided cannot stand, and that only when both house and contents are present to your awareness are you truly conscious and capable of really being involved in this miracle called life. So, work to remember yourself. Asking God to help you do this will help you succeed because it is impossible to remember yourself without remembering His Life, in which your life dwells.

Is there a relationship between living in the perfectly present moment and worshipping God?

Let me add this one idea to your developing intuition about the relationship between the perfectly present moment and the worship of God: This present moment *now* is where God expresses His Life. But that expression, and our awareness of it, are often two very distinct things. The more we can be awake in the present moment, the more aware we become of what we are in relationship with in the present moment. The natural need and love of God grows within us as an expression of all that we find in that moment.

I have been working to remember myself as frequently and for as long as possible, but I always fall back into thought and forget to try. Do you have any suggestions on ways to help keep myself from going to sleep spiritually?

Try to make a point to bring yourself back to an awake state as many times a day as you can. There are helpful ways to do this: Set simple physical tasks for yourself so that when you act them out, part of doing them requires you remembering yourself. For instance, at home or in the office, make it your aim to know you are reaching for the phone when you reach for it. When someone hands you something, come aware of yourself that you are taking it from his or her hand. Try turning off the radio or TV right in the middle of your favorite part—you will come awake! The more internal alarm clocks you can set for yourself, the more these helpful awakenings to yourself become possible.

The Promising Power of Being Awake

What is it about trying to come awake and to stay in this state that is so difficult to achieve?

For any person to awaken from the dream of self, they must fully come to grips with what is the "first-born" nature. This spiritually sleeping self is asleep in itself, to itself, and to the world all around it. It moves through life in a dream that it calls its life. This dreaming nature is content enough in its alternating nightmares and excitements. The key for us to understand is that our lives, as we know them, rest fully in the hands of this sleeping nature around whose neck hangs this sign: "Do not disturb." As we realize this actual inner condition of ours, then it isn't coming awake that is seen as being difficult when we actually experience how hard it is on us (and everyone else) to *remain* asleep. This new and higher form of self-realization is the seed of a new kind of inner struggle whose fruits (among many) may be counted in contentment, confidence, and compassion. Go to work!

I still seem to get caught up with my fears of the future: Am I going to reach my goals? Am I on the right path? I find myself going around in circles, and it always comes back to the fear. I try to remain in the present moment but the doubts seem to creep back in. What haven't I seen that I need to that will set me straight and stop all this self-doubt?

We each do all day long what we value. This is difficult to understand for the self that believes it doesn't want to fear; nevertheless, the fact remains that we involve ourselves in what our present level of self finds fulfilling. Now the answer here is to start seeing there is no value in fear outside of fear's promise to make us fearless if we will just do as it bids. As we work to be aware of any of these distasteful inner states, our very awareness of them not only increases our understanding of their real nature, but serves to help us lose interest in the feelings these states provide. It is a wonderful thing to begin outgrowing our own lower nature. It can be done if you persist in working at it.

I've tried to become more and more aware of myself, which has resulted in a realization that I am deeply asleep! I am beginning to see that I can't possibly have any "willpower" in this state of psychic sleep. Now what?
Your discoveries are accurate and will eventually serve your wish to be a whole person. One of the little-understood but essential steps in becoming a whole person requires discovering just how fragmented we are. We are, as presently constituted, little more than a merry-go-round of alternating selves, none of which knows the other. As this becomes evident, instead of acting out the impulses of these vagrant selves, our energies begin to be used to be aware of ourselves. It is this awareness, and in this awareness, that we find the whole life we seek.

As we work more and more at staying awake, will it get easier to stay awake and remain in the perfect present?
Always remember the following idea—it will help you through difficult inner times: This work (for many years) proceeds in two directions at once. For awhile, it will seem that you will find yourself feeling more asleep the more you try to stay awake. But if you will persist through these natural inner ups and downs, you will eventually reach the

realization that all of these moments (of either being more awake, or finding yourself more asleep) have been serving a secret purpose you couldn't have known about before that moment. All of your work serves to make you realize that unless the Supreme grants you grace, of yourself you have nothing. For years we try (necessarily) to possess the awakened state, only to find out the only way it comes into our life is to possess us.

> **Whenever it is that I come a little bit awake to myself, it seems I suddenly find myself feeling somewhat sleepy. I know it seems like a contradiction, but what is it that causes this dullness to come over me right when I want to be more aware?**

Every effort to awaken will cause the parts of you that want to remain asleep to throw at you the only thing that is in their power, i.e., confusion, doubt, fatigue, and the rest. Remember the following: All negative states are mechanical in nature and therefore bound both by time and the energy they steal from us to stay alive. Remain with your wish to stay awake. Be willing to bear the shocks and the natural reprisals from these presently unconscious forces. You will see these states eventually pass. Maybe this new experience of yours will help you understand part of the interior meaning of Christ's words, "Blessed are ye that are reviled in my name."

Enter Into the
Untroubled Now

Waking up to ourselves describes a whole new level of being self-aware. We no longer know ourselves simply through the thoughts we have about ourselves, but we can now see these formerly self-defining thoughts as being only one small aspect of who we really are. So it can be said that awakening *begins* with being able to see that we have been *asleep in the state of thought.* Looking at this same idea from the other way around, to be spiritually asleep means that we are not conscious of our own thoughts, and are convinced these thoughts and feelings are the same as us. This sleep state has far-reaching implications.

When we don't know we are in thought, then the choices these thoughts make can't be said to be *our* choices. This discovery explains much about how we often unwittingly choose our own undoing!

Now, add to this insight that our lives move at the speed of our thoughts. Suddenly we can see why we tend to crash as often as we do. There is no real driver aboard! Once this discovery is confirmed in us—through observation of it by a part of us that can see *into* this thought nature instead of seeing *from* it—we become interested in making a whole new kind of choice in life. We want to be awake to ourselves more than we want the comfort of the dreams that our thought nature creates. We are willing to invest more of our attention in seeing where we go to sleep to ourselves in ourselves.

When we will come wide awake, bringing ourselves fully into the present moment, thoughts cannot travel into it with us. With even a small willingness on our part to enter the Perfect Present, it is possible for us to experience the consistently new, thought-free, and untroubled Now.

In this higher, timeless realm, we are free *not* to do what we no longer find worthwhile. For instance, we don't have to relive our past again and again. We don't have to fear the future, because it ceases to exist as a fearful place in the true here and now. With all of this in mind, use the following special lessons and exercises to help you come awake and remain in the untroubled Now.

Whenever you do find you have suddenly come awake to yourself, your first inner task (besides welcoming this awakening) is to work to remain within this self-elevating presence. The difficulty is that this still, small, briefly awake part of you gets quickly overruled and run over by habitually sleeping "I's", effectively returning you back into a state of undetected psychic slumber. This is why, whenever you do find yourself a bit more awake than the moment before— wherever you may be, or whatever you may be doing— deliberately align yourself with this inwardly breaking light. Will yourself over to its will that you be awake. Seek ways to lengthen its stay within you by embracing these moments this awakenedness has brought you. In other words, do all that you can to *stay* awake.

One exercise in self-awakening is to begin to see that when certain types of thoughts or feelings pour into you, they bring certain preknown qualities with them that lull you to sleep in their welcome familiarity. When detecting these agents, voluntarily struggle not to go to sleep. Refuse to recline in the comfort of these habitual states.

Other inner practices may include deliberately speaking with people at an undetected (by them) fraction of your normal speed, so that while you are conversing, you will start to see and feel inside of yourself a whole host of thoughts never before known by you because of their formerly habitual pace and place within you. Through this now-conscious (to you) contrast—created by consciously slowing yourself down—you will be kept awake . . . and rather than falling to sleep, and into trouble, you will gain new strength and insights into the truth of yourself.

Whenever you can, and as often as you are able (right now, for instance), just come aware of yourself, of that to which you are inwardly connected. This awareness of what you are in relationship with in the moment instantly changes your relationship. Come awake over and over again in this way, and watch how new and higher energies, and their commensurate inner states, make a happy home in you.

four

Going Beyond the
Limitations of Thought

So much of the real world in which we live is invisible to us that most people are surprised to learn that all the usual forms of life normally considered as solid, or unchanging, are actually just the opposite. The truth is, nothing we perceive remains the same for too long, if at all. And this includes even the eyes that are reading through this text. The same eyes that started reading this sentence will not be the same ones that finish it.

In each human body—ocean of life that it is, with as many forms found in it as in any sea on earth—millions of its cells die every day. But even as these living organisms pass into oblivion, they are replaced through the miraculous process of regeneration. Some of these cells live only hours, some last days, while other more complex cells take a far greater time to run through this bodily cycle of cellular life and death. For example, science reports that some cells in our bodies may live for as long as ten years. And as these new findings come forth, solving some mysteries even as they reveal new ones, each breakthrough helps us to see ourselves in a new and special kind of light. However, and for now, these revelations do make one thing certain— and it is from this ground that we will prove the possibility of realizing a realm above and beyond thought.

Modern science reports that you and I, that is to say *our entire bodies*, are "replaced" every seven to ten years or so. This one fact alone, considered properly, can serve us as a kind of conceptual hub from which all manner of possibilities take off, all heading in different but orderly directions— something like a train depot serving rail lines that touch all parts of the continent. And we are going to head out on one of these lines of consideration and venture into that undiscovered territory within our own consciousness: the realm above and beyond thought.

Our journey to reach this distant High Country—whose Promised Land yet lies hidden within us—commences with this aforementioned fact of our continual physical becoming. If we realize even a hint of what is implied in this discovery, it can't help but change the way in which we see our existence and think toward ourselves. In turn, this dawning order of new self-understanding requires us to let go of many old and cherished concepts about our lives—one small example being that if we wish for something truly permanent in this life of ours, then our search for it will have to be made elsewhere than in our presently known reality. After all, who looks for pies made of sky?

And so, as paradoxical as it seems, our journey to a life beyond the confines of our own unconscious concepts begins with a strange and often shocking discovery: What needs to be escaped are the constraints of our own conditioned consciousness. In other words, the freedom we long for is from our present level of self that *thinks* the life it knows is the only life there is. We are, in effect, the unwilling captives of this level of self-consciousness, virtual prisoners of its unconscious conclusions. Our only hope of getting beyond its limiting influences is to outgrow it. This is why our search for freedom from our present level of self must include an expanded understanding of the entire cosmos that constitutes our individual physical, mental, emotional, and spiritual universes. Our next key point of study will clarify this last idea.

The new and higher self-knowledge that is required if we wish to transcend ourselves *cannot be realized through a process of thought.* The freedom we seek from ourselves is not an achievement of reconfigured ideas or any other refinement of our past experience, imagined or otherwise.

The true liberation of self comes to us in direct proportion to our awakening to a new and Higher Mind. This conscious level of Self dwells within a realm of understanding that no longer sees or experiences life along the habitual horizontal lines of time—with its endless chain of recurring opposites—but within the vertical dimensions of scale that intersect these lines of time and that contain them. *Don't let this last thought throw you.* It will take only a moment to show you that you have already seen a glimpse of these heavens above. As surprising as it is, many great truths we are aware of, we have yet to "see"—all of which explains the importance of truthful teachings such as these. They merely show us what was already a part of our own vision, but that we had somehow forgotten we had seen. So let's see!

Most of us have heard the timeless principle "As above, so below." This idea points to an ancient esoteric principle that each known world of Creation is itself a kind of smaller version or reflection of the realm above it. Imagine for a moment this idea of a cosmos within a cosmos by picturing a large tidal pool set next to the ocean whose ebb waters created it. Now, next to this tidal pool, picture a massive pitted rock just above the high-tide line in which the waters from a wave in the tidal pool have splashed and in which a small crab now sits. Here we can see how the lesser waters are always born of greater ones, infinitely. And though each subsequent realm of these waters is one in itself, it is still—in a manner of speaking—less complete, less whole then the world it mirrors, because each of these descending cosmos is a product of yet one further refraction or division.

What we now want to be able to see is that our present body, with all of its attending thoughts and emotions, is just one of these myriad cosmos. And further, that our body as a physical vessel—as complex as it may be—is still a "lower" cosmos, a reflection or animated manifestation of a far subtler yet more whole and higher body of Self.

With these last facts in sight, let's refresh in our minds the opening idea that this seemingly solid body of ours is always being replaced through the cycle of cellular life and death, that it is always becoming even as it discards what it can no longer be. So that—in spite of what our physical senses report—even this seemingly stable level of our self is not fixed matter. In summary: *Our physical body is not only what we have consumed, but it is forever being made over again from the stuff of our new choices.* And this brings us to the central point of this study.

If these findings hold true concerning the actual condition of our physical self, how much more so is this principle true, in scale, as it pertains to the ever-becoming state of our invisible spiritual body? Can we see that just as there are foods for the physical organism—some better, some worse—so too must there be, in scale, "food" for the spirit, for the soul? And just as our bodies grow healthy or not, according to what we take into our mouths, so too do we grow into wisdom, strength, or grace according to what we attend to with our mind.

When it comes to our spiritual being, every moment serves to either nourish within us the inherent freedom of Real Life, or it acts to negate this grand possibility and keeps us prisoners of our own unconsciousness. And if we had eyes to see into the secret realm of Self that sits behind the determining reality of our existence, we would witness therein that each of our thoughts, either consciously or carelessly embraced, forms within us the cells of our spiritual being. These building blocks of our supersensual "self" structure are what we call our experience of life, so that even as we think what we want to be, so are we made to become this self by the nature of these very thoughts.

But these insights reveal only a fraction of the story of our whole life possibility. Our thoughts, like all energetic life forms, attract to themselves natures like themselves. The thoughts of a fellow not only flock together, but seek and are sought out by similar invisible creatures. The implications of this discovery all point to one imperative: Our first action, our first choice in life—regardless of the circumstances life has put us in—must be to come awake within ourselves. We must work to be conscious of the nature of whatever thoughts and feelings are running through us . . . and for good reason. Here is why such self-watchfulness is so vital to our spiritual well-being.

Whether we are conscious of it or not, our prevailing sense of self is largely determined by the nature of our invisible interior relationship with these widely varying mental and emotional states. For upon whatever our attention is given, it is there that we stand inwardly, and whatever the actual nature of this ground may be—for the strength or shakiness of it—we share in that level of life. A moment's consideration proves this point and shows us evidence of this shared life.

All of our mental and emotional states are themselves in scale. It could be said that these various inner states we experience are really just reflections—or scaled-down expressions—of the myriad eternal forces that we embody. It is through these same pervasive energies, as they arrive and depart from us, that we derive the sense of ourselves that we do. For example, when gazing upon the beauty of a golden sun setting upon still waters, the serenity we feel is born of our momentary relationship with this timeless quality of tranquility. To the unconscious observer, it may seem his condition of contentment is an effect of a cause outside of himself, but this isn't nearly the whole story.

The truth is, our experience of this deeper serenity is a derivative of our awareness and where we hold it; in other words, our attention. In essence, *our awareness of any presence is that presence we are aware of.* Those forms we behold with our eyes—such as shimmering light upon a golden lake

—merely manifest this tranquil presence we experience. In this instance, through our awareness of the lake, we are effectively "practicing" the presence of these tranquil forces expressed there and are becalmed within by the bright waters. This principle of higher consciousness at work within us makes it possible to share in the nature of whatever presence we "practice" because our true, higher body is Consciousness itself. Our innermost nature is Awareness. *We already* are *the realm above and beyond thought.*

We have begun to see that our Real Self is a ceaseless, ever-changing, and vital expression of eternal energies, even though this timeless nature remains veiled from us because of our present level of consciousness. But we need not remain unwilling captives of this lower cosmos. We may choose higher. Our unrealized heritage is that we are entitled to choose what level of life in which we will live, and our as-yet unrealized power is that we may share this same life through conscious self-awareness. Or, viewed the other way around, we may decide what presence we agree to allow within us. In either case, think what this grand discovery means to those of us who wish to be free.

It is given to us to choose whether we dwell within the temporary or the permanent—whether we run with the stream that pours itself into the desert and disappears, or actively abide within the ocean that feeds all such passing pools. We are empowered to choose whether to give ourselves over to what hurts us, or to what heals us. In short, we may practice the presence of those states of being that are, in themselves, the source of our unconscious suffering, or we may work to practice, consciously, the presence of what is inherently filled with light—those elevated states associated with the Divine.

The key here is that everything depends upon how willing we are to be aware of the relationship between where our attention is and what we are becoming in that moment as a result of its placement. The unattended mind, by the very nature of the low level of thoughts such a mind permits, dwells in one unseen relationship after another with whatever punishing presence permeates this unconscious accord. If we will do the inner work to be conscious of ourselves in the present moment—to increase our awareness of all that moves within us in these times—we make it possible to give ourselves the greatest gift of life there is. We will share the presence of what is true, light-filled, timeless, and love-bestowing. We will reach the awakened life and enter our true home beyond the realm of thought.

Realize the Right Use of Thought

How can we use the mind correctly and begin using our thoughts to benefit ourselves instead of allowing them to cause as much trouble as they do?

Start with this: The real question here should not be "How do I empower my mind to think rightly?" but "What is it within my mind that is stealing my natural powers of reason from me?" Notice that runaway emotions cloud thought and produce a blur, a confusion, and a pain. This pain rushes to be free of itself and uses thought—any thoughts—as a train to escape itself. As best you can, drop the wrong emotions that enter into your thinking. In other words, don't allow them to drive the mind. Start with this inner work. If you will try this simple approach, intelligence will reveal itself, and its natural powers will come into play.

What is the role of thought along this path? Should we only be silent and observe, or should we also consciously use thought to investigate ourselves? It's obvious to me that there is something wrong with the way I think, but for the life of me I can't think toward the problem wisely. Any suggestions you might have about how to "get it right" in my mind and get on the right path will be appreciated.

Thought cannot resolve the problems created by thought. This would describe the wrong use of thought. But you mustn't throw the baby out with the bathwater. Thought can arrive at the logical finding that it creates both itself and the problems it would escape, and that to look to itself to release itself must be a waste of time. This reasoning is the right use of thought. Beyond this, thought is necessary for our practical use and some creative purposes. Left unattended, thought tends to become part of a machine that constructs a false self. Try to watch your thinking. If pain accompanies your thoughts, see it, and work to drop the thoughts responsible for the pain. They will tell you they are there to free you from the disturbance, but right thinking toward these states reveals that the pain is there because these same disturbing thoughts have managed to drag you into their disturbed world. The more you see the truth of your inner state, the easier it becomes to drop both the troubling state and the wrong thinking responsible for it.

Does it get to a point where you can tell the difference between the mind telling you something and God/Truth telling you something? How do you know the difference?

Start with the following idea, but understand that God makes His own rules: Higher answers, the kind that change us from the inside out, do not arrive via the same route that thoughts and feelings do. When Truth "speaks," there are no voices—only a special kind of silence that somehow tells all.

What is a good way to know the difference between who we "think" we are in our head versus knowing ourselves more directly through our hearts?

Sit quietly and become as still as is presently possible for you. Watch yourself. Work to discern the difference between thought and emotion. As a guide, practice shifting your attention from the content of thought that is moving through you to your awareness of yourself through which these thoughts are coursing. The discernment comes gradually. Work at this kind of inner watchfulness that allows you to see yourself more as the harbor of thought than as the waves that pass through "you."

How do we maintain a healthy balance between the following opposite modes of thinking: persistence versus flexibility? Persistence means: close mind, focus on the task at hand, decide, act, and accomplish. Flexibility means: open mind, look at the big picture, evaluate, learn, and grow. How do we determine what thinking mode is better?

Your question points to an important inner issue concerning the nature of thought: Why must persistence and flexibility be mutually exclusive? Think of water. What is more persistent and flexible than a stream? It is the nature of our present level of mind, the way our thoughts are conditioned, to only consider right and left, up and down, on or off. This is the real inner problem. Real intelligence is the marriage of persistence and flexibility. Our task, if we accept the inner work, is to place ourselves in relationship with this intelligence. Of course this requires awakening to, and letting go of, our mechanical modes of perception.

Many times it is difficult to distinguish which thoughts are true and which are false. Can you give some insights that will help make distinguishing between the two easier?

Here is a good way to begin to judge between what are true and false thoughts: Try to observe the difference between any thought you have (and this goes for emotions too) that either serves you or steals from you. Thoughts that serve us are of two natures: first, practical thoughts for our everyday living, and then second, higher thoughts that help us to understand ourselves and this life. Thoughts that steal from us are those that promise one thing and deliver another. For example, anxious thoughts always steal. They promise that, if we will obey their instructions, we will escape the punishment in the anxiety. These thoughts do not end anxiety, but keep alive the unconscious nature from which they arise.

Watching, Waiting, and Working Toward a Quiet Mind

I know that living in the Now is important, but what do I do with a rampant curiosity that constantly distracts me with interesting questions about everything?

Before we can make any real progress on the inner path, we must each learn what it means to be alone. Now this doesn't necessarily mean to be without friends, but it does mean that we must begin to become suspicious of the inner company that is always in tow. Sure, these internal visitors ask lots of exciting questions and fill us with all manner of excitements, but what we need to change in our lives cannot be found through company of their sort. As an exercise, and as a good way to tell whether or not the inner company you are keeping is indeed "friendly," spend at least forty-eight hours refusing to give your attention to the places they demand it goes. The task is to remain apart and watchful of what your thoughts and feelings want to drag you into instead of mechanically going along for the ride. To consciously abstain from these relationships that run you around is the road to being self-ruling. There is much to learn here. Persist.

It seems to me that sometimes certain kinds of thoughts just go through me, and I need to wait them out and not act on them. Learning to be inwardly still and just observe is a wonderful skill to develop. Do you have any further ideas on this?

You are on the right track. All mental and emotional states are forms of energy which, having entered the self, have no authority to remain of themselves. The more you are able to recognize the temporary nature of these states and the selves they create, the more you will begin to reside within—and have reside within you—what is increasingly permanent.

I like the idea of being able to see something or some-one without having to always derive a sense of self from what I see. How can I go further with this wish to stand apart from my usual way of seeing things and the self that it seems to create?

Seeing without "selfing" is a grand exercise. Through its practice, we can see how it is possible to understand our lives without having to use thought to interpret life for us. You can try this practice right now. Wake up and look around the room you are in. As you do this, see what you see while you remain aware of any thoughts going through you either describing to you what you see or defining the you doing this seeing. Now, can you see that you don't need these thoughts in order to understand the moment or the objects in it? If you will work at this simple practice, you will be able to meet people and events regardless of their appearance and be able to know what is right and appropriate for you to do in that moment without having to go into thought.

> In the morning, during my daily quiet time before the rest of the family awakens, I have much trouble concentrating on higher, spiritual ideas. My thoughts seem to race on about events from yesterday or what is coming up today. Should I continue trying to battle with these thoughts? When I just try to watch them and learn from them, they seem to eat up most of my allotted quiet time. It is very frustrating for me.

What you report about all the inner racket is natural for now, so don't battle this state. Instead of trying to impose silence upon yourself, give your attention to observing all of this movement in yourself. Here's a small truth that will help you win the real battle: All mental constructions have a limited amount of time they can stand without your support. Withdraw this support and wait them out. They will collapse, and silence will pour in.

I have wondered, as I try to observe my thoughts, if what I am "seeing" about them isn't just more thought-derived "stuff" that is keeping me there, captive. What's the best approach to getting out of this self-created cage?

Here is a helpful idea: Think of watching your thoughts much in the same way as a person who had never been to an aviary—and who didn't know anything about any species of birds—might spend the hour there. What is this person's experience? Here are all of these squawking, chirping, brightly colored creatures flying all over the place. She sees that they never stay in one spot too long. This observer doesn't have to know what these creatures are as she watches, because their behavior will educate her as to their nature. Watch yourself with no ambitions, and you will see what's what in the zoo called you!

Insights and Instructions Along the Timeless Path of Self-Knowing

The usual or sensual mind is always seeking experience. Its primary source of the food needed to sustain itself is the unconscious chain of reaction that constitutes mechanical, associative thought.

The hunger this nature has for this food is such that with each reaction there occurs within it a certain contraction that is both painful and pleasurable for it . . . pleasurable because this contraction creates a momentary sense of self, a false self created from being in opposition to what it considers. The painful aspect of this contraction is that all such actions cut off, or isolate, the nature in the experience of it—

which becomes a source of suffering for it in that this same nature also longs to reach a state of wholeness.

While experience may serve as the path to self-knowledge, still it remains the lesser half of the path to self-knowing. Self-knowing is not experiential. It has no one apart from itself. It does not take place in time.

Self-knowing requires risking the self that fears being no one—a "risk" that becomes an inevitable choice once the seeker sees that all pursuit of experience (whose root is secret self-confirmation) is powerless to bring an end to his sense of isolation and loneliness. Following are nine insights and instructions to help you begin placing your wish for true self-knowing over the experience-seeking sensual mind:

- The mind that asks "What's the best use of my time?" seeks forms of familiar stimulation (which it calls being industrious) so it never considers that what would be best for it would be to quietly explore its own self-induced desires.

- The mind that asks "What's the best use of my time?" is trying to hide from itself the fact of its own essential emptiness.

- The mind that asks "What's the best use of my time?" wants to *be*, and in its own agitated effort to become, fails to see that for it to exist at all proves that something already *is*.

- The mind that asks "What's the best use of my time?" will willingly pour itself into a thousand meaningless actions rather than see, just once, the futility of its own pursuits.

- The mind that asks "What's the best use of my time?" excludes, by the limited field of its own perception, the possibility that, in reality, there exists no time outside of its own point-by-point considerations; therefore, that there is no place to reach, no separate self to complete, and so . . . nothing to do.

- The mind that asks "What's the best use of my time?" can't consider that the best use of its "time" would be to see into the unconscious movement of its own thought process—one that creates not only the question of its own "best use," but also the self it needs to search for the answer to its question.

- The mind that asks "What's the best use of my time?" sees being alone and unoccupied as states having no value, to be avoided at all costs, because its only system of self-evaluation requires the ongoing presence of opposites.

- The mind that asks "What's the best use of my time?" is a mind in pursuit of those sensations produced by time, i.e., the sense of running from one point to another (from thought to thought) for the sense of self that this movement of time creates.

- The mind that asks "What's the best use of my time?" seeks experience, and because of its own conditioned nature is unable to see that what it really wants is the *unexperienced*—a state of itself that cannot be sought.

five

Breaking Out of Self-Punishing Patterns

Have you ever wondered, especially when it comes to self-defeating behaviors, why we must almost always reach our lowest point before we can make meaningful changes in our lives and in ourselves? What is it about these critical times in our lives that help turn us around, leading to greater self-understanding and its equivalent power?

The Chinese have long defined the word "crisis" to include the meaning of "opportunity." How different this concept is for most of us, especially when finding ourselves unable to outdistance some painful self-pattern about to overtake us. But if we can be courageous enough to take a truthful look at what the actual crisis is, forgoing our habitual reaction

63

of trying to change or escape the conditions perceived as being its cause, then perhaps we can realize just what a great opportunity these unwanted moments represent.

Let's begin this study by redefining the word "crisis" and bravely distancing ourselves from our current meaning of "reaching a critical point created by conditions outside our control." Our courageous new definition will be as follows: *A crisis is that telling instant when certain parts of ourselves— having already successfully deceived us—encounter the moment in which their deception is revealed.*

In other words, the real turning points occur (for us) each time something we believed to be true, to be real, is found out *not* to be what we had assumed. The financial deal, that special person, or some long-term relationship turns out not to be what it seemed; and further, we see that it never could have been what it promised. And it's right here, in the midst of our unwanted revelation, that we must dare to see what only the few and the true are willing to look upon.

Our ordinary interpretation of moments such as these is that it's the person or his or her default on a promise that is the cause of what punishes us. But we could never be in this position of going through the crisis of a deception *revealed* unless there wasn't, first, a deception *concealed*. And if you are confused at this point with where the author is headed, then add this old, familiar expression to your thinking: "It takes two to tango." Now, with this in mind, consider the following special truth, for within it is revealed the one true way to rise above finding yourself self-compromised and a captive of unwanted events:

To the one about to enter into it, no painful pattern starts as one.

Can you see the truth in this finding? How each unwanted circular condition of ours always has its beginnings in a hope, an expectation, an excitement? How, at its outset, the seed of each circle of self seems to be quite different from the bitter fruit it eventually yields? And since it's impossible that the seeds of a sweet fruit tree yield bitter berries, we come to our principle lesson. Before we can break out of any painful pattern, we must give ourselves over to the conscious study of its seed and not allow ourselves to be any further deceived by blaming the tree and hating the fruit it now bears. Condemning the unpleasant effects of an undetected cause is like shouting at your own shadow to make it go away while you remain with your back to the light.

Breaking out of self-punishing patterns begins with becoming aware of their real cause, which can be stated somewhat like this: Something within you that feels itself to be unsettled or incomplete identifies this unwanted state with something or someone that will, once possessed, provide you with a sense of being whole, complete, and at last in command of yourself.

This inner finding is important because we can all see, to some degree, that the seed, the start of some unwanted self-pattern, begins as an undetected thought or feeling of ourselves that instills us with a sense of our self as somehow being incomplete. Once this false sense of self sets in, the next steps fall into place automatically, mechanically. For now it is very clear to us: If we are *ever* to feel content with who we are, we must undertake the business of completing ourselves.

At first glance, this painful perception makes sense. But then again, as we have seen, so does each new deception we unconsciously agree to embrace. This is why we must bring new knowledge into the inner equation. Higher understanding—and the power of reason that surrounds it like a halo—creates a special form of inner light. It is the dawning of this light that breaks through our painful patterns and that shows us the way out of the circle of self. Here is a piece of this missing knowledge, the seed of truth needed to change everything:

We are not incomplete creatures, at least not in the way our sensual self sees itself. We are, however, *unfinished.* The difference between these two states of self is, as you are about to learn, immense.

In the "incomplete" view of ourselves, as provided for us by our thought nature, we must, compelled by our "own findings," seek our own completion or otherwise accept imperfection as our fate. It is *a priori*, given our incomplete state of self, that the "completing factor" *must lie outside of us, or else why would we need to be seeking anything?*

So in each new cycle of seeking we start out hopeful and excited by the idea of finally possessing what will, once possessed, allow us to at last possess ourselves. But near the close of each of these cycles we find ourselves not the ones who possess some new and rewarding sense of self, but rather the unwilling captives of the very condition we once dreamed might set us free!

Now, contrast the seed cast from *this* self, and the fruit it bears, with any real seed, be it seed of a mustard tree or of True Self. Seeds such as these are not incomplete, only *unfinished* relative to what waits within them. And there is more to this consideration.

What real seeds require to develop into their next form—whether sapling, full-grown tree, or self-conscious Self—is provided for right within their essential construct, as well as within the very ground into which they are sown. Everything needed to bear natural fruit is provided. Such seeds are patterned after fulfillment itself, and in their continuing evolutionary cycle they naturally assist other forms in their ongoing rise toward perfection. Reflecting upon the truth of these ideas is an important part of being rescued from the circle of self-punishing patterns. Here's why:

Breaking out of any painful pattern begins with seeing for yourself that any "self" struggling within you to escape some recurring negative cycle is the same one who, in its search to complete itself, willed this circle into existence in the first place. Only now its idea of feeling complete is wrapped up in the idea of escaping this trap it created. With this discovery in mind, add one last insight.

It is a lot easier to fall into a hole than to climb out of one, so stay awake to yourself. Catching and releasing the will of what feels itself to be incomplete, before it enacts its intention to go out and find its "missing half," is far superior to wasting your energies struggling as a captive of its creation. However, should you awaken one moment or another and find yourself a prisoner in some painful pattern already in motion, try to remember, as best you can, to add this last bit of light to your awareness of the moment:

Neither this incomplete self, its wishes, nor the circles within which it runs to complete itself *is who you really are.* To know the truth of this is the beginning of a freedom that can never be compromised.

Deliver Yourself from the Domain of Dark Thoughts

Once we have become conscious of self-wrecking thoughts, how do we know the difference between going into denial about them or otherwise unconsciously repressing them?

The only way it's possible to truly deliver ourselves from the punishment of our own self-wrecking thoughts is to begin awakening to their hidden cause within us. For example, self-loathing is a string of dark thoughts driven by negative emotions based in imagination about ourselves. The secret cause or undetected opposite of self-loathing is an unconscious image we have of being better than that self we detest. So it is not a question of repressing or ignoring self-wrecking thoughts and feelings, as neither of these inner actions will free us from the effects of unwanted inner states. Seeing beyond any doubt (or with doubt, if necessary) that the thoughts that attack us do so because we have unconsciously agreed to their onslaught is what makes us quit the whole business. In a manner of speaking, at this point in our inner growth, there is no more fun or hope left for us in this kind of suffering. Then suffering falls off by itself.

During the night (in recurring periods), I am assaulted heavily by many "inner voices" that finally subside by dawn. During certain specific activities (i.e., mowing the lawn, showering, etc.), I experience similar unwanted moments of feeling attacked. Why are certain times more difficult, and other times (such as dawn) so peaceful?

Just like there are creatures of the dawn, of the day, and of the night, so too are there certain "I's" that dominate certain times. It's good to start noticing this merry-go-round of misery-making selves. Learn increasingly to detect their appearance earlier and earlier, and you will begin dropping them sooner.

One maxim of self-development I sense is true is that the way out of any stressful situation is to "go through it." How does this approach apply to reducing stress-producing thought-attacks?

Everything depends upon our ability to inwardly discriminate between thoughts and feelings that are for us as opposed to those that are against us. Whenever confronted with an onslaught of internal impressions, the most powerful tool you have is to go silent. Step away from the situation inwardly by bringing everything that is going through you into your deliberate field of attention. There is a native unity in a silent mind that is able to both witness and "taste" the thoughts and feelings passing through it. It is this internal field of silence that reveals the character of any impressions and shows them for what they are. It's hard to make a mistake when your first wish is to see these thoughts and feelings instead of just unconsciously turning your will over to them.

I usually feel really good about things and less and less attached to the conditions around me in my life. However, sometimes I get thoughts (on a deeper level) that one might never imagine a positive person like me thinking, and they are possibly more negative than anything I thought of before my self-study.

Don't fight this new awareness. The wrong parts of us tell us that a "good" person doesn't have dark thoughts. This causes us to resist the state, which in turn breathes life into it. This is how we fall into the hands of negative states. It is trickery. Learn to watch everything and judge nothing. Stay quiet. All self-harming states must come and go if you will work at this. Lastly, in the light of these lessons, consider Christ's instructions to his disciples that they "resist not evil."

Where do all of these tormenting thoughts come from that we hear as voices within us? I think if I knew the truth of their origin, they wouldn't overcome me so easily. Can you shed some light on this mystery?

Rest assured that for now where these voices come from is not as important as the fact that they exist. Persist with your inner work, particularly working at becoming increasingly conscious of these voices, and something unthinkable will occur: Bit by bit you will be able to see into the nature (that does not belong to any individual) from which these inner voices of conflict arise. Like all ecological niches, everything has its place. Our place is within the higher life, where these voices either have no consequence or eventually disappear.

The Secret to Overcoming All Opposition

I think I must be crazy, but it feels to me as though one part of me wants one thing—for instance, that my husband treat me in a certain way—and that another part of me wants just the opposite, because I criticize him when he does as I wish. How can I get out of this trap?

No opposite within us has the power to cancel itself. What this means is that we must wake up and start working to see that it is impossible to release any conflict we may have by running in the direction it prescribes to escape it. As this realization grows, we begin to desire living from the truth within us that already understands that what we really want isn't a new direction in life, but to live from its Life. In other words, we must put aside all other concerns besides the one that directs us toward the Celestial Life. This is the way out.

Gradually I'm beginning to realize that my pursuit of pleasure and the avoidance of pain are the opposites of a single thought. How do I back up and see the whole thing in its entirety, so as to be free from this unconscious duality?

The understanding of the operation of the opposites is not an intellectual act. Using reason to try to escape the opposites, to negate them, is just the beginning of the understanding you need. In truth, using thoughts to address the problem of the opposites only compounds their confusion, as thought—by its nature—can only address one side of a thing at a time. True seeing is not a mental activity. The more you learn about the nature of the opposites, and how they are unable to resolve themselves, the more you will naturally step aside from their influences when they enter you. As you step aside—ultimately learning to see your life outside of these opposites—increasingly you will be able to see them in their original form.

There is much spoken about in higher spiritual studies concerning the "opposites," and how, for instance, we are unaware that to be for one thing often sets us against something else. Is this accurate? How does it relate to daily actions and decisions we must make?

The study of the opposites is very important in our inner work because it is the nature of thought itself to work in opposites. These workings are themselves in scale. The important point to be made here is that truly learning about the opposites requires being able to observe their operation within us, within our thoughts, in the present moment. For instance, all of us recognize the simple opposites of how a fear thought will produce a prescribed action to free us from the fear we feel. All such thoughts and imaginary escapes are really just the work of unconscious opposites and, when we take direction from this level of thought, we remain captives in the circle of self. But perhaps the trickiest of the expressions of these mechanical, mental opposites is that thought always divides the person seeing from what he sees. This is a deep subject requiring much study and self-observation; however, it is priceless for your inner development.

I find this hard to believe, but it seems that I must like my confusion because I spend so much of my time running around in it! What is it about confusion that attracts me?

Seeing that something in "you" likes confusion is the first step in bringing an end to it, but we need new knowledge to work with if we wish to finally get off of this sorry merry-go-round of our sleeping self. Consider this: Confusion is really a runaway play of the opposites, where one thought arrives at a seeming conclusion only to be replaced by another thought that calls it into doubt and then suggests another way to look at the same problem. The real problem is this thought-nature whose drive mechanism is the opposites, and whose secret intention is to keep alive the false sense of self that this internal dialogue perpetuates. See all of this and then dare to step out of this tornado of thoughts and feelings. You can't find freedom within it; knowing this helps you step outside of yourself. The point and the lesson is to understand that all that is whirling around inside you, when you are confused, is the contents of your present understanding, but if the level of understanding could resolve the problem, you wouldn't have had the problem in the first place. Growing to understand the truth of this higher view into the lower state gives you the interior advantage. Learn to act toward any confusion you feel with what you know is true about it instead of allowing it to draw you into an inner storm that can only perpetuate itself. Step back from yourself, go silent, and wait until the storm passes . . . it will. And on the other side will be a new understanding, both about what you mustn't do as well as what your next step should be.

Going Beyond Resistance into Life's Flow

How can I be sure that by becoming silently aware of some negative state of mine, I am not just secretly repressing this same dark emotion?

The continual repression of any negative state only serves to make it worse. Any form of resistance only empowers the state resisted. Working inwardly to become silent and watchful is not a form of resistance, but a deliberate act of involving your awareness with the intruder. This awareness will increase your understanding of the state until you no longer have any interest in it, and then it goes.

I find it very hard not to identify with my thoughts. Do you have any suggestions?

Many years ago, author Vernon Howard told a small group of students that "Resistance to the disturbance is the disturbance." This means that any thoughts or aspects of ourselves that we try to get rid of, i.e., the pain and the fear these thoughts cause us, actually keep us unconsciously identified with them. Try this: Instead of trying to push away troubling thoughts, see how deeply aware you can become of what these thoughts are doing to you, what they are causing to occur within you by their very presence. As you become more awake to the actual nature of these conflictive states, you won't want to continue your existing relationship with them.

Can you elaborate a bit on Christ's teaching of "Resist not evil" and how this applies to the movies playing in my head? Sometimes I feel like I'm looking at millions of them all at once.

Try to see it this way: Instead of concentrating on the various movies or scenes running through your mind, begin to notice the role, or sense of identity, that you are extracting from these scenes. If you will do that much, you will start to "taste" something completely different within the whole event. The movies (meaning the thoughts and feelings we have about what we see) are not the problem. Our resistance or attraction (which is secretly the same thing) is what we need to become conscious of. Your awareness and wish to have the Light/Christ's life as your own will begin placing you in a new kind of relationship with these internal forces. Your victory is in this new relationship, not in you trying to extricate yourself from what you see within yourself.

I can see how thought creates the opposites, especially when trying to control desire. The more I try to control my thoughts, the stronger the resistance. If you do nothing, then nothing changes. How do you get above the opposites?

What you must eventually see is that the part of you that wants to control desire is itself but an opposite of that desire you are trying to control. The only way to truly rise above the circle of self (which is what the opposites engender and perpetuate) is to see how certain thoughts and their habitual patterns serve to keep you secretly identified with this nature that is unconscious to and in itself. Stop trying to control runaway conditions and work more at being present to them within yourself. Letting go will naturally follow.

The Sure Cure for
Conflict-Creating Questions

The way in which our present mind knows itself and its surroundings is through the opposites. This isn't hard to see. Opposites are natural and necessary in the physical world. Up and down, left and right, sweet and sour—all help us find our way and guide our choices. But when it comes to succeeding in higher realms of reality, and winning their inherent rewards, this same mind, unconscious to its own dualistic condition, experiences certain consistent self-punishing limitations.

To begin with, this mechanical level of mind is only able to see life through the opposites. This means it is, in its very thought-action and perception, divided. And this discovery tells the tale. Here we learn that our present level of mind is incapable of grasping anything that is not one-sided. Consider the consequences.

For instance, whatever this divided-thought nature sees, it sees as being apart from itself. So any situation it looks upon, it views as being separate from itself. The problems inherent in this unconscious act of division are not obvious, although the pain it creates can't be missed. For instance: Anytime we don't know the immediate answer to some pressing question, this divided nature naturally concludes that the pain it "sees" in our heart and mind is there because of the absence of some sorely needed, but still missing, answer. Once having established this perception as reality it then seems only natural, and obvious, for this divided nature to begin seeking this missing answer as the rescuing agent for the pain it perceives. But what this divided mind can't see is that the conflict in its center is actually its own unconscious creation, conceived through its very own undetected, divided activity. A slightly deeper and different look into this psychological process will help clear up any temporary confusion.

There are times when we drive ourselves crazy looking for answers to questions when no such answers exist—at least as conceived of by *that level* of questioning mind. For instance, a frightened mind may ask what it can do about a scary situation, hoping to find an answer that will make it unafraid. This divided level of mind can't see that whatever it has imagined will empower it to become fearless—a new mate, more money, or enhanced social status—only secretly increases its level of dependency, and therefore, its fear. So, whatever "solution" it finds serves only to increase its own already agitated state. Let's take another example.

Maybe this same level of divided mind asks what can be done to get even with someone, as in wondering the best way to exact revenge. What this nature can't see is that its very own consideration of how to make someone else suffer only increases its own anguish—and that the real answer it needs is to be found within a higher, more compassionate view that it can't hope to arrive at because *this level of mind is unable to see both sides of anything*—for instance, how the transgressing party in question might have acted unthinkingly, without really wanting to have made anyone suffer perhaps, and most likely was driven along against his or her will by the underground pressure of some personal pain too great to resist.

But you can't be saying that, just because our present mind works in opposites, there is no answer for our pain?

No, not at all . . . only that there are some questions for which no answers exist because the level of mind that poses these questions is unable to grasp that *it is the pain it feels* when posing them.

I'm not sure I follow. How can there be questions that have no answers?

Let me show you. Whenever we get a stomachache, our internal distress begs us to ask ourselves the question: "What did I eat to upset me?" Clearly, for *this* question, there *are* answers. And should we realize our misstep, and proceed to obey our findings, the unwanted discomfort goes away. But in this example, both our pain and solution are physical in nature, which makes finding the cause and correcting the conflict a fairly easy task. However, in the subtler realms of our own psychic system, not everything we think we see is so clear-cut. Let's look for just a moment at the familiar pain of anxiety or fear. Psychological pains such as these incite us to ask, "What should I do about this unhappy moment?" But, as the facts are about to reveal, *it is this question itself,* and any other like it, which helps to produce and perpetuate our pain.

You can't be suggesting, are you, that questions we ask to resolve our aches actually cause our aching? Is that even possible?

In most cases, definitely! Our "normal" way of dealing with pain is to ignore it until we can't any longer, at which point this mounting pressure drives us to ask ourselves those familiar "What can be done about this?" questions—our perception being that coming upon the correct answer to the cause of our concern will eliminate the ache being felt. But the truth is, regardless of our short-term victories over these anxious states, they always return . . . unquestionable evidence that in turn reveals two other important facts worth our consideration:

- It proves that our present solutions to our stresses are not real.

- It shows that we have somehow misread the problem.

And so we have.

What we have missed seeing is that there are some questions which actually create the pain they seek to soothe . . . and that questions such as these have no real solution outside of being able to see them as false.

A good example of one of these conflict-creating questions that has no solution at the level of its origin is when that all-too-familiar thought pops up on the mind's screen and asks: "What should I do with myself to make my life more meaningful?" Consider carefully the details that follow.

Until the moment this "What should I do with myself?" thought popped into your awareness, you were not feeling anxious about yourself. But with this thought of how you might remake yourself in your own eyes came that same thought's invisible shadow—the fear of not being able to succeed as you have imagined. Now watch closely: As the pain in this fear takes center stage, so does your certainty that you must have an answer for it . . . which in turn only serves to drive the question wheel-of-worry around and around. And guess who's stuck behind the wheel? The good news is it doesn't have to be this way, if you can stay awake to yourself.

But before we go any further, let's remember that this special form of studying ourselves is not about analyzing our pains; no, this approach is doomed. We don't want to think about our stressed state; what we want to do is *to see* these negative states as they come into being within us. As the following insight helps to reveal, this difference—between seeing our states and thinking about them—is significant.

One of the favorite tricks of this false nature is that the pain it gets you to think about is itself being caused by trying to figure out what to do about it! Which also explains why, at least in these internal realms, the more clearly we can see into the operation of this divided, conflict-creating nature, the greater becomes our freedom from it. Now, let's summarize the points of this study section thus far.

If you don't feel disturbed until after some question appears in your mind, then it's that question which should be held suspect for its part in creating the conflict you feel. The key to freedom here is in being able to realize that this ache *has no answer* since the pain now pulsating within you never had a life of its own until that question, whatever it may be, breathed it into existence.

This cycle of sorrow is not unlike the sailor lost at sea who, unknowingly, or from sheer desperation, drinks salt water to quench his thirst. The more he drinks, the greater his thirst grows. Madness usually follows unless rescue and fresh water come first. This analogy is especially fitting because the Truth has long been compared to fresh, clear water. And so it is here that we must be willing to let what is true be our guide. Instead of mechanically trying to answer these conflict-creating questions at their level, which is to seek out one futile and false solution after another, we must dare to see into—and finally through—that divided nature asking these kinds of questions. Our new and conscious answer must be to drop both our worried concerns *and* that sense of self that these conflict-creating questions temporarily create.

I can see the wisdom in these insights, even if I don't fully understand them. Still, where do these conflict-creating questions get their beginnings, if my pain isn't their cause?

Don't be too concerned with this for now. Why worry about how to dive under water when you're just learning to swim? In time, with sincere study and a growing, quiet mind, all will be revealed. Let's just say that these conflict-creating questions can get started by any number of possibilities. They can include having their beginning in yet some other undetected pain, as perhaps born from the activity of unconscious associative thinking, such as when you see a new suit of handsome clothes in an upscale store window that you then, unknowingly, compare with what you have on that day. In a heartbeat you find yourself feeling terribly unfit and desperately inadequate. The next thing you know, you're asking yourself: "What is wrong with me that I can't seem to get ahead? What do I have to do to be a winner?" And in less than a heartbeat, the wheel-of-worry starts rolling along . . . and you're *under* it, not steering it.

Of course there are many more examples of conflict-causing questions that the divided mind can pose but not solve. For extra benefit, try to identify some of those more familiar questions that have you running nowhere fast! Just get started. Everything that you do to help yourself stay awake will also help to erase the ache of these conflict-filled questions that have no answers.

six

Turn Any Dark Condition into a Healing Light

There is a great and timeless truth hidden in the short statement that follows. Within it we discover not only why we continue to have the dark moments in our lives that we do, but also how we can use this very unhappiness to lead us to true self-victory. Once we realize what this truth tells us about our relationship with the unseen universe around and within us, we have come upon the power we need to turn any pressing dark condition into a present and healing light.

We are the subject of all that we have yet to realize, and the object of all that we have realized.

For the purposes of this chapter we will focus our attention on the first portion of this truthful idea: We are the subject of all that we have yet to realize. To help us understand this principle, let's first look over a few simple examples of how it works in our everyday affairs. We'll begin by restating the idea.

We are the subject of any physical relationship we are in that we don't understand. Perhaps the most obvious of these examples can be found in any form of addiction we may have had, or that we are struggling with at present. To begin with, no one who understands the actual nature of an addictive substance agrees to a relationship with it. Why? Because this person would realize, in advance of his actions, that to interact with any such substance is to become its slave, little more than an unwilling servant of what he originally thought would serve him. Without such knowledge he becomes possessed by what he engages, instead of being its possessor.

In the world of everyday finance, if we spend our wages chasing those endless objects of our desires, preferring short-term excitements over long-term security, aren't we subjected to the stress born out of spending more than what we earn? Of course. Here, more often than not, we find ourselves a kind of slave to the very possessions we dreamed would serve us. What has happened? These highly deceptive impulses (to shop 'til we drop!) promise us greater personal pleasure, even certain kinds of freedom, but their final result is to deliver us into the hands of debt, with its attending stressful states of fear or worry.

For our last example, if we haven't yet realized how our spouse, fellow workers, our children, or even our pets know exactly what "buttons" to push to get us to perform according to their demands, then we belong to them each time this happens. Again, it is our own unseen mechanical reactions that give them the strings to our mind and heart, transforming us into their unwilling puppets.

So it is a law: Whatever we have yet to understand about any given relationship in life is the degree to which we find ourselves the subject of that relationship, and all of our relationships with the world have their beginnings within us. Incidentally, though much to the point, on the flip side of this coin that represents our present level of understanding, we are, in effect, in command of any level of understanding that rests beneath our own. As just one example of this truth, consider that whenever two people meet, one will always naturally be "in charge" of the other, as this relationship is determined by which of the two individuals better understands the invisible workings of his own nature.

These valuable findings bring us to the purpose of this chapter's introduction. We are preparing to shine much-needed light upon our dark inner states and, according to the clarity of our insight, become empowered to dismiss the unnecessary suffering to which they subject us.

When we don't understand our negative states, when we have yet to realize how they trick us into doing their bidding, they have the power to make us jump through hoops like circus animals. It's not a pretty picture in which to see ourselves, but we must not turn our eyes away from these truths that are self-evident. When we are dominated by any negativity, be it some consuming fear or heated anger, we may think we are in command of ourselves as we rush to judgment or lash out at the world, but a simple question reveals another reality. Who, in his or her right mind, purposely sets themselves on fire? The answer is obvious. No one deliberately defeats one's own best self-interests. This much we all realize as being true. But what we don't understand, yet, is how we are getting tricked into serving these dark states. I trust the following is obvious.

Anytime we are taken over by a negative state, we suffer. In a flash, natural intelligence is replaced by ignorance; healthy flexibility turns into destructive rigidity. The fiery essence of these disabling forces imposes their will upon our own, and in a heartbeat our own actions can be unrecognizable, even to us. In short, to be in spiritual darkness is to hurt. It's that simple . . . almost.

When some inner turmoil captures us, the problem is that we will do almost anything to escape it. While this reaction makes sense on the surface of things—to run like crazy from anything that has the power to make us hurt—the truth of the matter is a different story entirely. *We can never escape any dark state that we run from because it's impossible to outrun the shadow of our own misunderstanding.* Think this truth through for yourself and contrast its finding with the following facts.

As any negativity starts to overcome us, our usual first response is to find a way to escape our rapidly growing discontent. In no time at all we come upon some mental course to set our compass by and then go into action. In each instance our habitual behavior can only mean one thing: Something within us, some unseen part of us, is insisting that we do understand our pain. But the truth is, we don't. We must not fear or dismiss this new and true understanding as *our suffering can only come to an end when we end our unconscious identification with the negative states responsible for it.* The only way to bring an end to our relationship with these unwanted inner states is to become wiser than they are! How is this done? We enter into a whole new *conscious* relationship with them—one that is based upon what *we* know is true about them instead of making our choices based upon what these states have told us is true about us. Now, rather than run from, or fight with, the punishing presence of some challenging, negative state, our new choice is to consciously challenge its right to our life. Instead of closing our eyes and going into daydreams of a better world to come, we deliberately come wide awake and allow that worried world pressing in against us to show us its stuff.

Perhaps you're thinking, "Who, in his or her right mind, would choose to engage such a formidable enemy?"—particularly one that has proven itself, time and again, not only superior to our wish for simple self-command but that sometimes outweighs our own best instincts? It is our largely unconscious consideration of this pivotal question—along with what amounts to our foregone conclusion—that brings our study full circle. Do you see what is revealed here?

Dark inner states win the day from us before we even know there has been a contest for control of our lives! How can we hope for self-victory when we have been tricked into surrendering ourselves before an actual engagement has occurred? And in case you're thinking this isn't true, please consider how we invariably submit to these negative states in one of two ways: First, we either fear their power and try to escape their wrath by hiding from them, or sometimes we just simply deny that they exist. Or, second, and no less counterproductive in the long run, we embrace the "guidance" these destructive thoughts and feelings offer us as to how we can escape their punishment by following out their rescue plans—an act not too dissimilar from asking the proverbial fox to guard the chicken coop!

In either case, what should be clear is that dark inner states win their victory over us because *we believe in them.* More to the point, we believe in the illusions they create within us without seeing that these same mistaken beliefs then shape the structure of our reality.

"But wait a moment. My pain isn't an illusion!"

"My fears are real!"

"If you suffered anxiety attacks like mine, you'd sing a different tune!"

No one is saying that our various dark inner states aren't real, and those who claim otherwise deceive themselves and whomever they try to guide. Such darkness is a reality, including the shadowy creatures dwelling within it. But the key to understand here is that this reality called darkness is itself but an effect of a far and away Greater Reality: the Light.

Here is the missing understanding for which we have been searching all along. Darkness, in whatever form we experience it—from a simple black, starless night, to a depressed thought or feeling—only exists in the absence of light. And the more clearly we can see the truth of this principle, regardless of the world in which it's expressed, the greater our potential to realize its power.

For instance, in moments where any dark state appears within us, be it in the shape of a fear, a worry, or a hatred of where life has led us, we must see that the reason its power grows over us—as it does—is because in this same time and space within our soul, there is no light present.

Stated slightly differently, and perhaps a bit more accurately, there is no awareness of the presence of light in us in these dark moments because, if there were, the punishing presence of that dark inner state would not be the sole basis of our reality.

The true solution for bringing an end to unconscious suffering now rests in our hands. The power needed to release ourselves from our unhappy moments is in the light of our new understanding as to how dark states keep us in the dark. In other words, to know the truth of them is our triumph over them. Now we must take these truths into action.

As a study in summary of this chapter section you'll find below a short list of seven special lights. Learning to call upon the new understanding they contain and reveal is all the help you need to dismiss any dark inner states.

- No negative state has the right to reside within you, and can only dwell there if it tricks you into lending it a dark room in which to stay.

- The Light is all the might you need to successfully turn away any dark inner visitor.

- Your true wish to understand a negative state initiates the entrance of that specialized Light you need to make this same wish come true.

- We suffer what we do, as we do, only through our unconscious consent, so the first step in freeing ourselves from unseen sorrow is to deliberately bring ourselves into conscious awareness of its dark presence within us.

- Never accept the presence of any suffering state for the reasons it provides.

- It is possible to understand any negative state out of existence!

- Your created nature is a blend of shadows and the light that creates them, but your True Nature, your original essence, is a Light that has no shadow.

Nullify Negative States with New Knowledge

I really have a difficult time dealing with negative states. Do you have any suggestions for what I can do to escape these dark feelings that overtake me so often?

One of the hardest things to understand about the spiritual path and the struggles along the Way is that the inner battle we fear losing has already been won for us . . . if we will choose the right side of the engagement. Our task is to stay in the battle long enough to see through the wrong parts of ourselves that are producing both the negative states and the experiences these states produce. If you will learn what it means to endure until the end (i.e., to stay awake to these states until they pass—which they must, being the mechanical forces they are), you'll find yourself on the next step of the path above you. You'll know you went higher because you saw through and let go of the lower. Here is a clue as to how this will work for you as you do the necessary interior work: Negative states linger only as long as they are fed. It is a fact that no negative spirit or thought can stand alone. This is one of the most empowering inner discoveries a person can make along the path. This realization is why we must learn to be alone, and at the same time why if we will accept the truth of what we see within ourselves, we are simultaneously set free from both state and self.

When I try to walk away from my familiar sense of self (which I admit tends to be a bit brooding), it seems like my world turns dark. I think and feel this darkness in me in a literal sense. Worse, I can see its effects on others around me, but I have no sense of balance or direction in these times. I feel lost. What's going on?

Have you ever gone into a darkened room and not been able to turn on the light? And then if you stayed there, you gradually began to be able to see what you formerly were unable to see? A natural part of you, asleep at first, was able to awaken and give you night vision. This is a parallel. Remain conscious of this darkness. Don't let yourself derive a sense of self from it. The light will come. Then you will know what to do in all such instances.

I'm starting to think it would be a good idea for me to learn something about anger, as it always catches me off-guard, whether the outburst is in another person or myself. What are these secret fires that live in all of us, and should we seek out angry situations to better understand them?

Our work must be with what is, not with what isn't. What this means is that to go out looking for self-destructive, negative states is like seeking your own hand. These conditions coexist with this life as it presently is. So we mustn't go out to "find" suspected self-defeating states, but learn to bear consciously their appearance within ourselves when they surface. Life provides the field, we just have to be there. As for some indicators of anger to watch for, like smoke before the fire, learning to observe impatience and intolerance of ourselves and others will ultimately prove rewarding. Watch these states closely. They will show you what sits beneath them.

> I can sometimes go for two or three weeks without suffering from overt negativity. Then, out of the blue, I will have a day where bad thoughts and feelings move in and through me in what feels like a persistent attack. What is going on? Is this natural? What should I do?

There are two sides to this story. The first is to understand that everything in the physical world moves in cycles. These alternating states are naturally occurring waves of opposites. The second fact to understand is that our work is about transcending or outgrowing the mechanical cycles of our physical world. As we develop, we learn to let go of this earthly self that is so bound to these cycles. Stay awake. Then work harder not to express these negative states, but to quietly see them in operation.

> I can't believe that I still choose to let dark emotional states such as rage or anxiety into my inner house. Sometimes I even see these dark clouds coming, and still I give myself over to them. I'd like to be stronger.

There are certain vital shocks that each of us must go through if we want to become a different kind of human being. One of these critical shocks is the discovery that we are indeed possessed by what seems to be two wills. Recall that the New Testament apostle Paul said, "I don't do the good I want to do, instead I do the evil I don't want to do." What he was pointing out is that it's one thing to come aware of a conflicted nature, and another thing to begin being able to not express it. The ability to not express negative states is not a power we win. We are freed from these conflicted inner conditions as we die to the nature that is their progenitor.

The Power to Eliminate Dark Emotions

Could you give some insight into loneliness and how to abolish it?

Loneliness is not the problem. *Fear* of loneliness is what drives us into wrong relationships, including despairing of ourselves. Think about it: The feeling of being alone has no negative content in and of itself. But as the mind works on it, and brings to bear all of the past negative experiences about being lonely, suddenly loneliness turns from a lamb into a lion. We can never be free of any negative state without being willing to meet it, to see it fully. Negative states continue to win the day and our lives because they know we won't look at their face. One great spiritual secret is that if we will dare negative states to do their worst to us, God will take our defense. This means we will see through that state.

Lately it seems to me that the more I try to work at being a better person, the more alone I feel. What's this all about?

I know it seems strange and even unfair that for our efforts to be true human beings, we often feel as though we are being punished. Did you ever hear the expression from the New Testament, "Blessed are ye that are reviled in my name"? Christ told his disciples this, but what isn't specifically stated in the Bible is that this is both an outer expression of a person's work and an inner one. This is important. The pain we feel—whether it's aloneness, emptiness, fear, or whatever—that arises as a result of our efforts to win Real Life is not an effect of that Real Life per se, but a kind of reprisal from our old nature, who uses the only weapons available to it to keep us in line. As this truth gets clear to you, your intolerance with these kinds of inner threats will grow. One day you'll laugh in the face of all such painful feelings, and your laugh will be rooted in reality.

I am in a situation with two competing fears: the fear of being alone for the rest of my life, and the fear of approaching and speaking to someone new. Any action I take seems to be giving into one of these fears. Is there a way out?

Try to see that it isn't being alone that frightens you. What is scaring you is the movie that runs within the theater of your mind called "My Life Alone." The only way out of this movie is to go into the aloneness, understanding that the fear you feel about it is a lie. If you will do this, the movie ends, and with it the wonder and pleasure of what real aloneness brings.

What is the source of severe depression, and what is the most effective way to begin attacking it?

We have to see the big picture in order to succeed with our wish for freedom from any state. All things physical have gravity. This includes thought-forms and emotional energies. All thought-forms and their accompanying energies operate under the law of association and attraction. Depression begins with an unconscious act of identifying with certain images about ourselves. These images or ideas usually have to do with pictures we hold in our own mind about what we are supposed to be or accomplish in this life. The problem with this set of ideas is that they don't belong to us—they are an effect of the world we live in, whose nature it is to measure ourselves by values passed along by others. When we compare ourselves unconsciously to these ideas and fail to measure up, it just drives the circle of self. First this nature looks for itself and, failing to find what it's looking for, it simply returns to its own content for another answer, which is always part of the problem and never the solution. Now multiply this and you will understand severe depression. Since this negative state enters us and takes possession of us in our unawareness, new awareness is the solution. In order to see what we must about this false sense of self, it is necessary to investigate it instead of giving ourselves over to it. Don't fight with it. Add as much light (awareness) to it as you can, and it will begin to lose its hold on you. And here is one additional thought: As you lose interest in any negative state, i.e., in the sense of self it surreptitiously provides you, the state dwindles away into its native darkness, no longer a problem for you because you are no longer a place in which it can dwell.

Elevate Your Life Above Loss and Grief

What, if any, is the relationship between this growing sense of sadness I am experiencing of late and my growing love of truth studies?

The sadness that seems to appear along the Way belongs mostly to the lower aspects of self that are unable to take the next step. What this self grieves over is not what it says it does, but for the end of itself. On the other hand, as we awaken and see the unnecessary pain and strife in our fellow creatures, there is born in us a certain kind of sadness over this great waste. This new empathy, which feels like sadness at first, signals the birth of compassion.

I have read that grief over the loss of a loved one is only the suffering of our false self. If so, is there such a thing as grief that does not include the idea of loss?

Don't believe all that you read. There is such a thing as natural grief. Losing a loved one, a truly loved one, cannot go without effect. The key here is to be awake and not take part in grieving over one's self at the loss of another. This is where grief is not only "a lie," but unnatural, and leads to long-term unhappiness in the continual reliving of the loss. There are certain invisible laws in this world of ours, one of them being that everything passes, no exceptions. And when we invest our sense of self in that which passes—when that thing, possession, or person changes—we feel first a fear and then a corresponding sense of loss because we have mistaken its life for our own. Suffering follows.

Someone I was deeply in love with has left me after several years together. I am crushed. I have dated others,

but none compare. How do I pull myself out of these obsessive thoughts about what I once had?

The sense of self that any suffering produces is guaranteed to find ways to continue that same suffering. Try to see when these sad thoughts come to you and invite you into their world that they always promise you something. Connect the pain that follows your entrance into their world with their presence, and eventually you will see through these lies. To help you refuse this insidious invitation, ask yourself repeatedly: What good is anything I may possess that when I no longer have it, I no longer have myself? Stay with this question (and its intent) until something in you awakens that wants its own life more than the false life provided for it through temporary conditions.

I have been a Christian almost all my life. A few years ago I had to have open-heart surgery, which caused a stroke, messing up my ability to do my job. I ended up losing a job that I was good at and enjoyed thoroughly. I feel like Job in the Bible in that I have lost everything because the thing I did best was taken away from me. I have always heard that when God closes one door He opens another. I find myself getting down and not knowing which way to turn. I try to keep my faith, but I feel I am losing. I try to live in the present moment, but find that it is getting harder to do.

God never forsakes the soul that loves Him . . . never. The problem is, our souls (as they presently are) lack spiritual understanding. We think we are who we think we are, and these thought-constructed natures—these images we hold of ourselves—are in a form of enmity with God. For these reasons, when God gives Himself to us, we often don't understand the gift. Take Job, for instance. His trials and willingness to endure them, in spite of everything, did not confuse his love for the Almighty. Why? Because he knew in his heart that God is good. Sure, His tests may be tough, but for whatever reasons, God only gives tough tests to those whom He needs to be tougher.

Why did God, in His infinite wisdom, create a situation for humankind that would allow for so much pain and suffering?

Apart from evil, suffering is the least understood subject in the world. You may have to ponder this for a while, but think on this idea: Has not the suffering of someone you love not invited you (at least) to make a change for the better, if not actually led you to that change?

Nurture Your Unshakable, True Nature

I am unhappy with my weight gain, lack of exercise, etc., yet seem unable to change it. Every time I start to make real progress, a setback comes along and brings me back to square one, filling me with doubts and self-loathing. What should one's attitude be toward these setbacks? I do want my health back, but I feel stuck.

It's possible for us to learn to use anything. *Everything* can be used. This is the secret of self-awakening. One of the biggest tricks of our negative states is that they secretly conspire to convince us that what "is" is all there can be. This conclusion belongs to who we have been, and can't touch who we may become if we will just gather ourselves up and start life all over again. Remember that who we *really* are is always becoming whatever we agree to be, so don't allow *who you have been* to draw you into agreeing to remain the same.

I know there must be a relationship between good physical health and true spiritual principles, but what part does truth play when it comes to our healing?

Everything is in levels. When it comes to our bodies, healthful and true dietary and physical regimens are important. But the real issue rests with invisible forces operating beneath or beyond the physical. No body can be any healthier than the energy it conducts and embraces. In the long run, real health is a question of relationship. Our task is to wake up to those unhealthy inner relationships we presently are involved in so that in discovery of them they can be replaced with higher and more balanced elements. Healing naturally follows each new healthy step that we'll take in this manner. And incidentally, healing is in scale—not only as it concerns our physical well-being, but our spiritual nature as well. There is no end to God's health!

When I am in physical pain and not in control of what my body is doing, is there a tip you can give me for easing the seemingly inevitable anxiety?

In one sense, everything about this life is a kind of preparation for death. This death that is inevitable physically is one indicator that we should be using its long shadow to find ways to stand in the light. As strange as it seems, it is this fear or resistance to our own physical end that perpetuates our painful relationship with it. It is hard to understand, but if we will not run from this fear, but rather become intimate with it, we will grow so tired of being afraid that we will die to the fear. Dying to this fear is the real beginning of dying to death. This is something you cannot have explained to you, but rather it is a bold inner requirement we are all given the opportunity to realize. If we will refuse to run from the battle we face, whatever it may be, victory appears!

Increasingly, I hear strange ideas like I should learn how to embrace my own pain, or walk into my own "shadow-self." Does this mean to accept the very unhappiness that I'm working so hard to be free of?

Accepting any negative state does not mean welcoming it. It means simply to allow Life to teach you what it wants you to learn through whatever relationship there may be at the moment. Life is not throwing questions at us; it is giving us answers. This is one of the greatest secrets in the world. Real answers are complete. Our task is to start understanding this. If you will do your inner work, you will be shown everything you need to know.

I can make myself sick with just the simple thought of a certain painful memory crossing my mind. Is there a way to defuse the hurt instead of sinking into it?

The next time some hostile state takes over your life—either in thought (as in remembering something someone did to you in the past) or in an actual moment of conflict with someone standing before you—ask yourself the following question at the moment you can remember yourself to do so: Is this self that I am presently experiencing the me that I want to be? Or: Is this suffering self how I want to know myself? And then just come as awake as you can to the realization that you are not who you want to be at that moment, but that something foreign to your True Nature has imposed itself on you and taken over your life. Then, once having done this, do nothing else except realize that while you may be temporarily powerless to stop the lower state from possessing you, you are empowered to recognize the negative state as an intruder. This awareness—this conscious awareness of your true pained condition—is what it means to put the light on the problem. That is your job. The light will do its part, if you will do yours. Persist until you are free!

Wake Up and Be Free of Fear and Worries

Before speaking to someone who intimidates me, I sometimes feel my throat start to close up and my voice choke up with so much tension that I find it hard to speak. I've got to get behind this fear, but I don't know how!

One way in which it's possible for us to outgrow the problems that we face is to not let those problems dictate our behavior to us. In this instance, whenever we run into areas that are challenging, a part of us will urge us to avoid those situations that make us feel uneasy. The answer is to go into the problem, not let the problem take us away from seeing its real cause. The wrong parts of us are always defining us according to their secret limitations. In this instance, anything that we fear, or that makes us behave oddly, will tell us that it's the person or the situation that is causing us the conflict. We must always remember that in all circumstances, *our situation is ourselves*, and that it is through direct contact with these parts—and doing what they fear to do—that will prove to us there was nothing real in the fear. All fear, all negative states, are conditional. This means that if we will stay the course, and be willing to remain aware of ourselves while these parts are threatening us, we will see them fade and disappear. This is the only freedom.

I have a lot of fears about an event I am planning— what to serve, who to invite, etc. How do I know if these fears are irrational or if I should listen to the voice that is telling me not to hold the event at all?

All psychological fears are, in a sense, irrational. Start there. If you want to have a party, have it. But don't let the party, any part of it, be at your spiritual expense. There are two ways to proceed, and both require your inner work: Have the party (and exactly who you want to come to it) exactly the way you want it, but make up your mind that you will not entertain tormenting inner guests as you make your preparations. Do this and you will learn more about yourself than you would if you decided not to have the party. Or, cancel the party and watch for the same uninvited inner guests.

In spite of some of my spiritual progress along the path of self-liberation, whenever bad news arrives via telephone or mail, I still face fear. My heart pounds, I forget everything true, and find myself right back where I started from. What can I do?

Strangely enough, waking up to discover that we have forgotten what we thought we knew is the beginning of a new and higher kind of knowing. Let me explain: For many years, we meet thought with thought, events with right principles. But higher thoughts and right principles are still the same level as the attacking state. We must learn this the hard way, which gradually allows us to stop fighting, stop resisting these negative states. We are not trying to learn how to over-power darkness, we are learning to dwell inwardly where darkness can't touch us.

> **Anxiety seems to be my lot in life lately. I have a full plate of activities with children, a challenging job, and outside interests. I really feel like I balance these and keep my priorities straight. However, I am visited often by anxiety that seems to have been triggered by worry. Do you have any suggestions on how I can work through this?**

Anxiety is one of the more difficult internal states to work with because of the way it works within us. The key is to begin realizing that the only influence any anxious state can have over us is in what it promises us we will have if we will do what the state tells us to do. One of the important aspects of your inner work is to begin learning deeply to recognize these individual states as they invade your psychic system, and in the beginning (if nothing else) to meet these states—especially anxiety—with what you know is true about the state instead of listening to what the state tells you is true about you. The Truth wants you to understand that anxious states live for themselves at your expense. The clearer this becomes to you, the freer you will be from giving yourself away to any anxious state.

> **I am starting to see where this planet is heading. With wars raging and me in the middle of it all, will my spir-itual work lift me out of the clutches of this dismal place? And if so, where?**

Freedom from this raging planet, with all of its wars, begins with discovering and walking away from the war within ourselves. In truth, there is no other battle, and what we see around us is the inevitable expression of the pain within us that pushes and pushes until it finds some release. As far as where your spiritual work leads you, leave it to the Spirit. It will never betray you.

The Way to Defeat All Dark Forces

What is it that keeps people in their psychic sleep? Does the devil or any other spiritual force contribute to this?

Yes, there are deliberate forces, inherent as themselves (and dwelling in matter) that work to keep us asleep. Try not to divide this idea up into parts, but see it as a whole. Everything wants to remain as it is. Everything wants life. This includes those forces and spirits whose life depends upon keeping us from seeing this truth.

If evil forces need my unconscious cooperation in order to steal my life and manifest themselves through me, why are they dedicated to my destruction?

I know that it seems, on the surface of things, to be a lose-lose situation for the darkness, but you must understand certain aspects of scale. Even the virus that would consume the human body doesn't perish when the body it has consumed does, for it belongs to a deeper order of life that is in a sense eternal relative to the temporary forms in which it thrives. The same holds true with negative forces.

Is it true that when we place ourselves along the higher path and begin to make real progress, evil deliberately tries to sabotage our spiritual efforts?

Yes, our work to embrace the Light naturally attracts opposing forces, however, there are spiritual truths that can transform these seeming adversaries into emissaries of the very Light we seek. For now, remember and work with the following idea: When any darkness comes upon us and attacks our wish for a holy life, it always betrays itself by revealing itself. In each of these revelations, if we are awake, comes the collapse of where we were unconsciously in relationship with these dark forces.

It is so much work to do and be good, and so easy to fall prey to dark forces wanting us to stay asleep. Doesn't this make it seem that darkness is somehow more powerful, more natural even, than light?

Try to understand that we are in a physical realm in physical bodies, both of which are under certain laws (i.e., gravity) that make it easier for things to fall down than to rise up. This physical condition and its inherent darkness that is an effect of being clothed in matter is not the ruling power for anyone wishing to rise above himself. The only power that darkness has is in the absence of the Light.

Three New Choices That Dismiss Dark Conditions

The only thing most of us know to do when life takes an unwanted turn, bringing us what we don't want, is to take a turn for the negative ourselves. And when the circumstance in question really makes a wreck of things, not only do we summarily reject the event seen "at cause," but for good measure we often will turn our wrath upon our own lives, pronouncing them "not worth living"!

Such flashes of frustration born from our growing sense of futility make sense on the surface of things, and even seem curative to the self that feels so impossibly stuck. But a closer look proves otherwise.

What many have yet to understand is that dark, negative reactions to unwanted events do nothing to cure them. In fact, these painful impulses have just the opposite effect. They actually "cement" things—fixing both themselves and the false sense of self through which they then are empowered to run their unhappy course. Here is some help to see the truth of this.

Each negative response that passes unconsciously through us actually confirms its own dark perception that life has "done me wrong"! But this is only half of its occult operation. This same conclusion—of having been somehow victimized by an uncaring world—virtually locks the door on the possibility of ever discovering the real lessons and the truth behind these times of trial. Whenever life runs counter to your wishes, try to see that it really isn't life that has denied you your happiness, but that the real culprit responsible for darkening the moment is some idea you have about what you need to be happy.

Admittedly, this new and higher perception takes courage, because instead of struggling to change the "dark" condition called into question (or just silently stewing over it), you must turn and face the false self responsible for this outlook. But the truth is there is really no alternative, not if you can see that as long as this demanding self stands unchallenged within you, so will the painful pattern of fighting with unwanted events continue to occur. The next time that life comes knocking with what you "don't want," instead of allowing yourself to be dragged through the old round-around, make these three new choices, and watch how they dismiss the darkness knocking at your door:

Your first choice (always!) is to come wide awake to yourself. Remember: Your new aim is to not allow old, mechanical reactions to rule the day. Then, in this awareness of yourself, see that the unpleasantness of the offending moment is not actually in the event itself but is an effect of resisting your own perception that something has taken away your happiness. Key here to escaping this circle of self-perpetuating punishment is in coming awake to its existence, and how not wanting to feel a certain way is giving you the very feeling you don't want!

For your second new choice, stop complaining to yourself (and others) about what life has "done" to you. All you are really doing is recreating the very dismal state-of-self you are condemning. Consciously choose to go the other way, which brings us to the third and most important choice in this exercise:

Say "yes" to life. Instead of blindly refusing moments that seem contradictory to your contentment, and then arbitrarily pushing them away, learn how to embrace these unwanted moments. Bring them into your real life, into the light of self-awareness, instead of trying to get rid of them. Your conscious embrace invites these times to tell you about the self they help to reveal. Freedom follows.

seven

Cancel the Secret Cause of Self-Captivity

A wild stallion was captured and put in a wood-fenced compound bordering the open country in which he once ran free.

His first week in captivity he showed all the wildness of a once-free creature now penned; but in the weeks that followed, even the dried grasses once refused as food became not only tolerable but even agreeable. After all, no effort was required on his part to eat his fill. Food and water just appeared daily. And there were other benefits, it seemed.

While he was unable to get out of his compound, neither could anything get in; so his formerly restless nights, long disturbed by the fear of his predators, had now become just an old, bad dream. His new situation seemed to him more and more a kind of trade-off, and not that bad of one either.

Some unknown time later, a wild stallion ran across a neighboring hill, near enough to spot his captive cousin. Cautiously he approached the pen. "What are you doing in this strange place?" he asked as he looked around for any sign of trouble.

"I'm trapped," said the captive stallion, between bites of his dry feed.

From outside the gate the stallion impatiently pawed around the gate's wooded posts. "This gate looks flimsy. If we both run into it, you from your side and me from mine, I bet it gives way. You could escape. What do you say?"

"Thanks, but it's not worth trying. We'll just both get hurt," spoke the captive horse as he pawed the worn ground of his pen to make his bed for an afternoon nap. "Besides, I've already tried it and nothing gave."

The wild stallion flared his nostrils and snorted out, "I can see from this side that the wood in this gate has rotted. Let's try!"

"No thanks," the captive stallion sighed as he lay down, considering a roll in the dust but deciding against it because his water trough was too nearby. "Besides," remembering the bruises to his shoulder, "I ran into that gate a dozen times, so if anyone should know what shape it's in, I ought to. Trust me," he added with a last measure of certainty to his neigh, "it's no use."

With this the blood surged through the heart of the wild stallion, who lifted his front feet high above the gated fence and then back down, raking the gate, breaking off pieces of the rotted holds. Then, fighting back his growing longing to run from this desolate place, he spoke once again. "When did you last test the gate's strength? Or your own?"

But the captive stallion could barely hear him. He had already slipped into a deep sleep where he was dreaming, once again, of open plains, grassy fields, and running in any direction his heart wanted . . .

Whenever we find ourselves in some "unwanted" part of ourselves, perhaps reliving an old heartache or caught in the throes of some irrepressible anger, old fear, or unyielding worry, part of this unwanted moment includes our certainty that we're trapped in this condition. And compounding our confusion over feeling ourselves captive in this way are all of the attending negative inner voices. They tell us not only are we hostages of these disturbing states, but that the pain we now feel will be with us forever.

Perhaps we rally ourselves for a run at the gate, refusing to accept our ache as the only possibility. But the more we charge toward the perceived cause of what holds us captive (the gate in our stallion's story), the more we bounce off it, or worse—our pain can actually increase, amplified by the mounting frustration of our thwarted wish to be set free.

Bit by bit we come to accept what we see as the inevitability of our unhappy, captive condition. And should we hear from a still, small, free part of ourselves, "Try once more, you don't belong there in that cell of yourself," from within us rises a chorus of negative voices to drown it out—a choir constructed from our own past experiences that sings out, "There's no use." So we go to sleep within ourselves, preferring to dream of better times or in the imagining of what we will never know outside of our fitful reveries. But we can wake up! We may awaken from not only the unsatisfying dream-life into which we've slipped, but from the unconscious dream-self that would have us remain there as captives of the lies it weaves. Shattering this dream world—and its hold over us—begins with bringing real light into it. This needed new light comes to us, first, in the form of new knowledge—an insight such as the one that follows into the actual nature of these negative states and the self they capture.

Regardless of the assertion of any negative state that seeks to convince you otherwise (using its painful presence within you as "proof" that the prison you're locked within will stand until the end of time), apply this one great truth:

All punishing self-states are "lies." They must break down if they don't succeed in breaking down your willingness to test their reality. How do you conduct such a test? You learn to look at their presence within you with the quiet understanding that, in reality, nothing in life is fixed. All things change. Everything passes. This is truth. Knowing this to be true is power over what holds us captive.

On the other hand, according to another great truth, everything in life tends to become more of what it is, so that the only things "fixed" in us are those parts of our presently unenlightened nature that convince us to resist life's natural changes. As this fear-filled, downward-trending nature tricks us into accepting its conclusions, they become the same as our captivity. We unconsciously accept the limited and painful life this alliance-in-the-dark produces. We can do better!

Real self-change begins with seeing that Real Life is change itself. This means there is no condition that can hold you captive without your unconscious cooperation. With-draw it. Wake up. Walk out of yourself by changing how you see what you call your life. Realize that while the contents of your life may come and go, turn dark, or suddenly seem delightful, regardless, these things will pass. Resting in the awareness of this truth while working to stand upon its higher ground, you come upon the Life within you whose nature is the unchanging witness of these movements. This Self dwells outside of change, even as all that changes moves through it.

Clear Away Common Problems and Frustrations

I need a better understanding of how to approach daily problems. How can I move from desperately trying to escape a problem, to a passionate desire to understand the right way?

Problems can't be escaped, because what you look at as a problem is really a mirror. Understanding this unseen rela-tionship between the difficulties you face and what you are produces a whole new paradigm. Instead of struggling with what is little more than a psychic Chinese finger puzzle, where the more you pull the tighter the trap draws, you learn to let go and relax from both the perceived problem and the self stuck in it. This new understanding not only stops the wastage of your precious life energy, but helps realize the love of Truth.

Pertaining to self-development in the workplace, why would someone keep saying and doing things at work that self-sabotage, knowing it will just get them in trouble, i.e., putting foot in mouth, doing personal business, etc.?

One of the initial and most difficult barriers in our growth is the discovery that within us are a diverse number of selves or "I's" that are completely opposed to our development. It is the discovery of these self-limiting selves that is the beginning of the end of them. Until we recognize their existence, we take their guidance as being true. Once we see it's not, the Truth itself fills the gap.

I feel like I'm stuck! I need some kind of new motivation for doing things that I just don't feel like doing, even though I know I need to do them. Where do I look?

All procrastination is rooted in resistance. The mind imagines how unpleasant a task will be by comparing it to past tasks, and then resists its own comparative findings. If we are asleep to this inner dynamic, we unconsciously accept its findings and are defeated by it! Try doing what you don't want to do by going into it with a wish to learn something new about it. Newness is life's principle. On the other side of resistance is the flow of Real Life.

I am becoming more aware of negative traits within me that I am expressing even though I know I shouldn't. This is very frustrating. Do you have any suggestions?

Stay in the battle. Where did anyone come up with the idea that self-liberation is possible without paying through self-

sacrifice? We must understand the need to surrender ourselves. Our false nature isn't going to take this idea lying
down, but the only weapons it has are shadows.

> I have recently had an experience where, in the aware-
> ness of a personal problem of mine, I came to a real
> understanding of it. In a flash it just didn't bother me
> as much. Shortly thereafter, the same issue over-
> whelmed me for the whole week. I just couldn't find
> my former understanding. Will this continue to occur
> until I really see the truth? Am I not seeing something
> about myself?

Let's start with this: There are always more, or higher levels of
ourselves, waiting within us to be explored and made our
own. So of course there are certain more subtle elements of
our own existence we have yet to see. Still, what you are seeing now is vital to your development. First, the discovery that
you are not the "transformed" person you took yourself for is
a vital lesson in seeing how your thought nature steps up and
unconsciously takes credit for everything: It says "Now I'm
this," or "Now I'm that," etc. But real inner changes are not at
the level of thought. Each time something unwanted pops up
in us that we were sure we had left behind us, we need to use
these recurring moments to see that we were deceived as to
the real nature of change. Then, the next go-round, we will be
more awake and far less apt to identify with what we take as
being ourselves. This new kind of nonidentification represents another, still higher order of change.

Beyond Temptations, Bad Habits, and the Addictive Nature

Could you explain what you think is the best way to create good habits or eliminate bad ones?

Here is a short poem: "Thoughts turn to acts and habits are born; from habits the shape of character is formed." We drop self-defeating behavior by coming awake to the fact that each negative act to which we give our life is first a bit of life stolen from us. It is not well understood, but before it is possible to defeat ourselves, we are in unconscious relationship with a defeated nature that is not our own. By working to be awake to ourselves in the moment, our awareness of these destructive energies permits us to actually experience their dark nature *before* that nature has a chance to deceive us. And how does it deceive us? With its promise of relief from the very pain its presence within us has produced! Once you can see this truth, you will also see that all self-defeating acts are the effects of our unawareness. Awareness ends this downhill relationship.

Recently I have been shocked by what I see is a growing fascination with a kind of sickness running through our whole society. What is it about violence, fear, and gore that seems to thrill us?

Within each human being dwells the full spectrum of Light and darkness . . . all energies co-inhabiting. Our fascination with evil, with violence, belongs to those dark aspects of our present nature that actually feed themselves and are sustained by this enigmatic energy. Stay awake. Detach yourself as best you can from this relationship with darkness. There is much to be learned. You are safe as long as the Light remains your preferred friend and innermost wish.

I have been working with the nonresistant approach to a troubling habit. As I work, it seems that every time temptation attacks, it lasts for shorter durations of time and doesn't attack as often. Will the temptation eventually cease attacking altogether?

All things move through life, and through us, in a kind of special bell curve with predictable durations. Temptations will have times of being easy to disavow, and then turn around and be, seemingly surprisingly, almost impossible to handle. All this is to say that yes, the "attacking" forces will diminish if not fed, but stay awake and don't fall prey to the idea that you are now stronger than the habit. The only real way to be free of any problem is to outgrow the self that finds some value in it. While the following ideas aren't the whole answer, within them is some higher help you may use to win this inner war: Bad habits have the hold they do, in part, because when we challenge their right to wreck our lives, their response is suddenly to seem more powerful. The key here is that this habit has not grown stronger in these moments, only that we have become more conscious of its dictatorship. This new awareness is the seed of our gaining the strength we need to overthrow this tyrant. For when we are tired enough of living beneath its dark domination, we will drop both this habit and the defeat it engenders.

It is easy for me to try to let go of negatives such as anger or worry. My problems come from the ones I like but that get me in trouble, such as excitement,

anticipation, etc. These I know are also false but some-times so much fun. How do I give these up?

Consider this simple truth and how it holds true in all levels of life: "The child finds the classroom when he or she tires of the playground." What you are really saying is that the temp-tation of an exciting sense of yourself presently outweighs your wish for a deeper relationship with that which doesn't lose itself to any moment. What we must all do is work increasingly to stay awake in all such moments and, by this kind of self-remembering, begin to "taste" more deeply these exciting states. There is nothing wrong with a good time, but not when the cost of it is the compromise of our conscience. Staying awake, coupled with your continuing work, will eventually lend you the inner force necessary to remain detached from these or any other troubles.

What do I need to watch for in myself in order to get past certain persistent and, at times, pernicious temptations?

Here is one helpful insight you can begin to work with: The first temptation can be traced back to our incomplete nature looking for some way to find a sense of feeling itself complete. However, everything it finds—because of its own temporary nature—is itself, by necessity, temporary. The response of our false nature to this endless cycle is to reinvent the next thing to fulfill it. Frustration grows, and the process speeds up. Under-standing this circle of the false self enables us to begin the process of detaching ourselves from these uncomfortable and recurring feelings that we must find something outside of ourselves in order to be whole. The true solution isn't to go out in search of some imagined wholeness, but to rediscover the whole state of our Higher Self.

Addictions come in many forms—substance abuse, people abuse, financial addiction, sexual addiction. Are some good and some bad? What are some higher thoughts concerning addictions?

There is no such thing as a healthy addiction, just as it should be clear that—in reality—there can be no such thing as any pleasure we are compelled to seek and give ourselves. Anything one part of our self does to drive another part proves the presence of a deep divide within us, where we are at once the slave seeking to escape and the master who releases us only to catch us again. This is, incidentally, one of the hidden aspects or characteristics of all unconscious thought.

Releasing Guilt, Blame, and Resentments

After certain negative events take place—especially in the company of certain people—I am almost overcome with the feeling of wanting revenge. I think I'll regain my peace of mind if I "get even." How do I free myself of these troubling thoughts?

Thoughts of revenge promise to relieve the mind they occupy of the very pressure these same thoughts produce. All acts of revenge are not only useless, but destroy the one who acts from them. These are not just words. If you will refuse to give dark thoughts and feelings your life for a long enough period, they will reveal themselves to you as being the secret destroyers they are. I promise you that such negativities have no life outside of the one that they steal from you when you act from them. Work at this until you see the fact of these dark forces. They don't bring the freedom from the pain they promise, but only compound your inner conflict.

What is the best way to make up for wrongs you have done in the past to others (betraying, lying, stealing, etc.)?

All of us have wronged others. Truth be known, until we wake up, we are all—in one form or another—in some kind of wrong relationship in life. That is why the key to correcting what we consider to be a faulty past is to work to be awake in the present. The wrong parts of us want to keep themselves alive by continually dragging before our mind's eye all that we have been wrong in doing. Then we react to these images and—in one form or another—resist them. All this unconscious act accomplishes is to secretly continue the life of this mistaken perception and the wrong behavior it perpetuates. Drop all of your concerns for what is no longer, and be intent on being conscious of what is before you. This changes things.

Is there any value to clearing away the wreckage of the past? It seems to help, yet I feel wrong in trying to correct so many mistakes that are behind me.

The wreckage of the past exists only in the thoughts of the self that keep it alive. Work to make things right in the here and now. Come awake to the pain in rehashing regrets and you will see yourself revisiting the scene of a "crime" long past. These scenes are the nightmares created by a sleeping self and are kept alive by remaining asleep to yourself. Learn to prefer your fresh awareness of the new moment over your frustrating memory of moments gone by. Do this special kind of inner work and the healing you want will follow, which includes the healings necessary with, or in, others. This is a spiritual law.

What about the idea of repentance? On one hand, being repentant for ourselves—as certain old religious teachings say we should be—seems as much a part of being self-punishing as is just "cutting loose," going wild, and then feeling terrible afterward for our reckless actions. Is there a true repentance beyond this idea of just living full of regrets that change nothing?

Let me offer this: True repentance has nothing to do with any ideas or images we may hold about ourselves as either being "bad" or "sorry" for what we have done. Real repentance is an unmistakable, instantaneous moment of insight where we see, to our shock, that something untrue, unjoyful, and self-destructive has been living our life and getting us to call ourselves—and know ourselves—by its presence. Lastly, this shock—and what it brings—leads to the birth, or the discovery, of a new kind of inner peace that has no opposites.

The Wisdom to Escape the Circle of Wants

Most of us, on a day-to-day basis, go though life carried along by a constant stream of expectations. In fact, these expectations are so common to our sense of self and its well-being that we barely even realize we have them until we run into something that dashes them. For proof of this, haven't you ever been surprised at how upset you can become over the smallest change in how someone treats you? Or what goes through you when, perhaps, the street you usually take to get to work is closed for repairs? Seen from this vantage point, our lives reveal at least one great truth about the way we see events: *Almost anything we encounter that is unexpected is usually construed as something negative.*

This discovery has far-reaching implications for anyone wishing to walk the spiritual path, because—simply put—the heart and soul, foundation and rafters of the true spiritual life is the *unexpected*. Let's take a closer look at this finding.

We have all had those moments in our lives where something unexpected came to us and, pouring itself in, left us breathless . . . perhaps as simple as rounding a bend and catching sight of a distant, breathtaking vista, or just being in the right place to see the play of last daylight on waxen leaves waving their yellows and greens within shadow-drenched trees. Maybe there was something in that special stillness of an early morning that said, without words, "All is well." Or, for those so blessed, Grace herself made her always-welcome, unexpected appearance.

In these surprising moments you see that there *is* another world, another life. You realize that whatever you had thought yourself to be only the moment before is not the whole story, and that there is so much more. Everything shifts and for a moment the former is no more. The new is all there is. And in this unexpected light something blooms in you. Here is where the true seeker is born.

But perils and promises often arrive together. Without being awake to yourself in these transformational times, an unseen want is born within you, a longing to relive or gain control over your uplifting experience. And, in the same instant as this desire takes shape, another expectation is created.

Let's put these important lessons together, beginning with the realization that each desire for some spiritual grace creates the expectation of the desired. If you can see the truth of this, then you are also able to see these next two vital discoveries:

First, this same expectation effectively keeps you from those experiences that can only come *unexpectedly*. Second, until you can recognize and release these parts of yourself at the root of this unconscious inner runaround, you are trapped in a circle. Let's review.

To want is to expect. To expect is to know. To know is to have already experienced. To have already experienced is to live in the past. To live in the past is to be a dweller of a mental circle. To dwell in a mental circle is to feel as though you are closed off. To feel yourself closed off is to live with a sense of being incomplete. To live with a sense of being incomplete is the secret source of all wants. Round and round you go, but you are never going anywhere! Here is the new knowledge you need to escape this circle of wants:

Even though we often speak of it as being the "higher life," the authentic spiritual journey is not so much about a direction in life as it is about an *expansion* of it.

Whenever you have an expansive moment of understanding, it is *you* that is opening up, entering into something that was always there, and that will always be there . . . forever continually becoming more of itself. This new self-understanding is like finding yourself within a beautiful sphere of light that is always larger than you are, even though it is within what you are. And within its new revelations are your new intentions, new energies, new everything. This unfolding process of infinite possibilities is a miracle. It is in you, yet you are in it, and the whole affair is always new, never expected.

The following easy exercise will help you escape the circle of wants and to realize the truly new and unexpected life.

Each day, make it a point to spend some time in a natural setting. Never mind that you "don't have the time." If you want to find your way out of yourself, *take the time*. Go for a walk in a park, or just go outside where there's sunlight and trees, maybe some birds or squirrels. To receive the unexpected, learn to invite it.

Look at life around you. Don't sit there and think about it. See it. See the way a tree stands, the way a leaf falls, how sunlight streams across a road or field. See that nothing is static in life other than your own thoughts about your life. Just let go of your familiar self. Dare to drop your longings, your expectations about your life in favor of being willing to be alive . . . and welcome the unexpected. Come wide awake to yourself. Then quietly *know* that all around you—in every living thing, and within you, in your life itself—there dwells an ever-expanding universe telling its story to those who will stop and listen for it.

As you work at this simple exercise, what you want from life will begin to change. Why? Because you will come to see, increasingly, that *what you want already is yours*. There is nothing to chase, nothing to pursue. There is nothing that can be held onto because not only is it clear that all of life is ever-enlarging herself, but to hold onto anything limits what you can have. The birth of this understanding is the beginning of the way out. Take it.

eight

Lessons Only Love Can Teach

Part of the contentment in any pleasant surprise comes with the fulfillment of our desires and, in these moments, being granted a measure of peace from these deeply seeded longings. But hidden in the heart of each such moment are the secret seeds of our next longing. This truth is evident enough, for in less than no time we are on the go again, creating new wants and wishes needed to satisfy our newly arising passions . . . such is life. So it's not really news to us that when it comes to the ever-changing seasons of surprises, all of them hold elements that are almost always sweet *and* sour. Yet . . . it's not *always* so.

Once in a great while we stumble upon a whole new order of being surprised—one that doesn't arrive on the heels of a marching band for us having won some worldly prize or otherwise achieving a goal, but in the quiet fire of some undiscovered promise about our self. Here, within us, is uncovered a secret of self so luminous, bearing such great tidings, that this new discovery does the impossible: It somehow fulfills us with the very longing its promise has awakened in our soul. Conscious in us now, unleashed to its own purposes, is a hope for things unseen—a silent promise of Spirit that, if carefully followed, leads us directly to the timeless fulfillment to which it points. I am speaking of Love, and of all her many unrealized relationships.

However expressed in us—from the lowest level of sensual life pushed along by pure desire, to that incessant drive to make ourselves special in the eyes of the world, to those loftier ambitions of longing to be an instrument of the creative life, whatever its form, be it lower or higher—it is Love that moves us. It is Love that guides us. It is Love that we seek and find. How? Because it is Love in one of her endless interior forms that sends us to seek her in one of her many worldly disguises. The Lover and the beloved are two motions, one breath—an eternal affair animating not only all of Creation but whose secret source is the essence of our very being. And evident in this invisible romance, for those with eyes to see, is an unparalleled mystery—one that has perplexed humankind since the beginning of time: Love is an eternal flame, but there is no substance of earth that can satisfy her supernal fire.

In this fact resides one of our greatest unseen fears. For it is only while Love burns in us—which is only while she has the "soul stuff" she needs to combust—that we feel ourselves *truly alive.* But Love is as relentless to this stuff of our soul as is the brush fire that rips through a field of summer-dried grass. And when there is nothing left to feed her, when there is no more material remaining in us to enflame, it isn't Love that ceases to be, but it is we who feel ourselves flicker and falter. For just as fire without fuel has no reason for its being, without Love we have no reason to go on living.

Surely we have all gone through those dreaded times when it feels like we are dying because our heart is emotionally starved for life. Perhaps we have reached the end of our hope for some pivotal relationship, or come to the close of another goal that again proves itself to be empty. Whatever the cause, our passion faints and, with our wings suddenly clipped, we fall back to earth. We have all felt this fear, but few have seen its dark face up close. Its shadow taunts and haunts us in every fire we race to build or by which we hope to warm ourselves. For life has taught us—over and over again—that even the most carefully maintained of these fires eventually loses its warmth and light.

These moments are typified in the experience of finding ourselves having grown cold to a former close companion, or in seeing the light in their eyes wane in its warmth toward us. Or perhaps we have lost interest in our once-cherished career or lifestyle, so that no passion remains in us for what had been our sole and guiding purpose in life. But we must not (as we so often do) confuse this growing chill in our heart as the death of Love's fire. Love never dies. She cannot. She is life itself. The cooling passion we feel toward what once enflamed us is not the end of Love's fire, but only signals that we have now consumed all of the stuff of self available *at that level of ourselves.*

It may help to see this new idea by visualizing the action of actual physical flames as they move about in a fireplace. See how all open flames reach ever upward. See how they rise to ignite *what they are created to consume.*

Now, see that Love works in this exact same way. But the difference is that Love burns her way up, and through, the stuff of self. First, as an unwelcome visitor, she burns through our vanities. Where before we were warmed by glowing images of ourselves, Love shows us all that glitters isn't gold. And as her fires move through this lower soul region, they take with them—in their purifying path—our self-fascination. But in the very act of first enticing us with this ego-centered love, and then through expiring this same stuff of self in her compassionate flames, she accomplishes two feats at once:

First, her fires remove an interior section of our self's sub-flooring once felt by us as being our entire foundation—an act whose gradual consummation feels to us to be the loss of our life itself. And it is in this moment of our heart's cold confusion that our part in this eternal play is called onto the stage now set within us. For here, time and time again, we must choose whether to close ourselves off from Love's internal action—or offer ourselves over to it.

We have all seen the effects of shutting out Love: A hopeless frost clings to the heart, choking off higher emotion until only a shrunken shell of its former self sits there in place of the heart, its own beating a punishment.

And we have all had some level of experience with Love's successful passage through our various life stages—how the seeming loss of one love (or passion) first creates a sense of emptiness that is followed by the hope and promise of yet a deeper or wiser one, and then—although impossible to glean in the moment of such a sense of loss, and yet through this very loss—how Love reveals a new place within us for her next and higher incarnation.

This is how Love works her magic. This is her timeless motion and miracle. But we must agree to move with her according to her secret ways. We must each learn what it means to open the hearth of our hearts to her mystical fires and not to fear the stages through which she will take us.

If we consent, then ever on and upward will her flames work their way through our passions and take with them, into the air of their origin, our hopes in self, our hopes for things seen, and sometimes, in dark nights, even our hope for Love herself.

But if we agree to stay the course of Love's action in us through the passage of time, even though it may be often hidden in the residue of ash and smoke created by the upward passage of these living fires, the next level of Love is revealed to us. Herein we stand in amazement upon a whole new floor of what we now realize is our own self—a floor previously hidden by the self below it in a nature that could only be burned away through experience. Like the phoenix we rise again, ready to live out Love anew . . . and, hopefully, enriched by wisdom, ready to die again for the sake of Love.

Finding the Love You Long For

I often find myself longing to be in love. Are human love and relationships something we should strive for, or are these needs just some strange device of our false self looking for ourselves in all the "wrong places"?

Pretending not to have a desire can be a desire worse than the one it replaces. If you long for a relationship and the love that comes with it, then fulfill your wish as best you can. Relationships are precious. In them we learn not only about the inner life of others, but through them we are able to wake up to our own inner nature. In the long run, the whole of this life is a special preparation for Love. We come to this higher Love through all of our relationships in life, but in particular, through our personal interactions with one another. It is through these relationships and their lessons that we are ultimately purified of all secretly destructive self-interest.

From many spiritual sources I have investigated, it seems I get the same message. They say, in effect, I will never find love if I go out looking for it. So how do I stop my mind from wondering if the right person is just around the corner?

Don't try to stop it. Instead, be increasingly interested in what your life is actually like, moment to moment, as you wander through life waiting for someone to make you whole. There is no such person that can make any of us whole the way we dream of this kind of wholeness. Unfortunately, we have to go through these stages of "looking for love in all the wrong places" before we realize it has always been right within us. On the other hand, and this is one of the paradoxes of the spiritual life, our relationships are essential to helping us discover this very fact.

It never fails that I always get too emotionally attached to my significant other—an attachment that usually drives this same person away. How do I maintain a healthy, un-needy relationship without pushing the one I love away from me? I've tried to act like I don't care as much as I do, but my facade always breaks down, and my relationship with it.

Don't try to be anything to your friends (male or female) other than allowing yourself to be what you naturally are. Pretending that we don't need someone doesn't change the essence of the relationship they experience with us. Ultimately, everyone meets us as we are, not in the way we want them to see us as being. Besides which, there is nothing wrong with wanting a lasting relationship with someone special. Where we go wrong is in falling prey to those parts of ourselves that tell us without someone special to be in love with, we can't have our longing for love satisfied. This isn't true.

At times it seems to me that the more I realize about the awesome nature of spiritual love, the more loneliness I feel in my current human relationships. I long to share my discoveries with others, but who do I turn to?

A certain kind of loneliness, of feeling ourselves all alone, is a necessary portion of the path to the higher life. This sense of being alone comes out of realizing what are the inherent limitations in our actual relationships in this life, combined with a growing spiritual longing to commune with others in a deep and meaningful way. Go through this. We easily forget that there is a God, a Great Intelligence that guides the steps of anyone willing to put Him/Truth before all else. This same Intelligence will lead you to new relationships, inner and outer ones, in which not only will you be able to express the love you feel for the Truth, but this same love will fill you as well.

Can a person choose the path of Truth and travel it through life with someone, or must they go it alone?

The answer is that we must both go alone and at the same time allow all relationships to reveal that, in truth, we have never been alone. Having a loved one who loves the Truth with you is a great blessing because the two of you can learn to give yourselves up to a greater Love. So ultimately, surrender becomes the key. We can learn to let go of ourselves more easily when we have others around us who show us the need for this self-release without punishing us for our transgressions. It is a curious thing: Sometimes it is much more affecting when someone doesn't blame us for a pain we impart than when they do. That is the beauty of inner work.

In a relationship, how do you give yourselves up to a greater Love without being codependent?

Giving ourselves to a greater Love *frees* us from all painful codependency. Whenever two people put the love of Truth, of the Almighty, before themselves, their love will flourish in ways impossible for those who have only themselves to either embrace or blame. To help clarify this liberating fact, try to see the truth in the following insight: Where two people believe their happiness is in the other person's hands, therein you have not only painful codependency, but something of a more insidious nature. You have two people who have closed the doors to the possibility of knowing the divine Love that brought them together in search of itself.

The Many Levels of Love and the Lessons They Hold for Us

How many levels or types of love are there for people?
The Greeks have four words for love: *eros*—romantic love; *philia*—brotherly love; *storgé*—family love between parents and children; and then the most powerful, *agapé*—love based on principle. For our purposes here, we can say there are two kinds of love: The first is the emotional type. This is the love that we all are given to know and to work with by our very creation. This love is good, natural, and provides the basis from which it is possible to move into the next or higher order of love. We can define this higher love, for now, as being an inclusive love in that it is impersonal. The principal difference between these two kinds of love is that the emotional love arises from and tends to create the self that loves. It is always a form of identification. The higher love that originates from God's love feels no need to possess what it loves because this love is whole and complete in itself. In the New Testament, Christ asked Peter repeatedly if the love Peter had for him was of this higher nature. Peter didn't understand the difference between his love and the one Christ spoke of, and his denial of Christ (moments later) revealed the difference.

How can we begin the process of transcending our own limiting self-centered love to come into a fully conscious and impersonal one?

One of the most shocking and necessary discoveries along the path is that what we love does not love us. We are filled all the time with powerful feelings and emotions that seem to lift or otherwise provide purpose and self-worth. It is not too much to say that most of these inner states are lies. By this I mean that these feelings are hopelessly incomplete of themselves, and so seek completion in some secret opposite that they generate. As we grow and become weary of finding ourselves, only to lose ourselves again and again, a certain spiritual clarity comes that makes the source of this betrayal clear. As it does, we fall out of love with ourselves. In proportion to this detachment, real Love reveals itself within us as having always been there.

Can a loving, true friendship between a man and a woman exist without physical attraction or sexual desire? Is this kind of love impossible?

Absolutely there is such a thing as true friendship. Physical attraction and the "love" it produces is an elementary stage of higher love and can help lead to it. In the varying stages of later levels of this higher love, the two people involved are self-completed and therefore don't look to one another to fulfill a sense of incompleteness, however manifested.

What is it about loving and being loved that makes it seem impossible to live without—and yet (at times) impossible to live with. I'm so confused!

In many ways the whole of this life is a special kind of preparation for Love. We begin this endless relationship through our various associations with people and the sacrifices and learning lessons these relationships both provide and demand. But in the end—meaning as we ready ourselves for our own further inner development, and the deeper, more fulfilling relationship with love that attends each of these steps—we come to an amazing finding: The more we would possess anyone or anything, the greater the unconscious sense of separation we experience. As this becomes clear, and our need for love continues to grow, we come to an astounding revelation: What we really want is not to possess, but *to be possessed*. What our heart is seeking it finds in giving up the self that strives for love. And in its place, love—real love, timeless love—appears.

> All the great teachings speak of a strange relationship between falling out of love with ourselves and self-awakening, and how these two conditions occur in us at the same time. What, then, is the role of self-love or self-esteem in our lives?

Think about this: What is love if not unity? Harmony? Now ask yourself, what is the state of someone who has to think about herself in order to feel valuable or loved by herself or anyone else? Can you see that such a person is unconsciously divided, therefore feeling incomplete, and that her very nature suffering from this state of division then tries to embrace itself? The result is the insatiable appetite for self-assurance through self-reference.

Exploring the Realms of Higher Emotional Energies

I have come across repeated sources, some of them ancient, that say sexual energy is the greatest power that we possess. If this is true, how can it be channeled?

Trying to work with sexual energy before you can understand and work your way through simple mental energy is like thinking you can tame a bucking bronco before you have mastered a sawhorse. Before you try to harness these particular passions, try to rein in something as simple as being impatient with others. It is critical for any person attempting real inner work to not get tricked into believing he can do something real prior to his understanding of reality. This is where so many fail, and then fall—all because they thought themselves to possess certain strengths when, if the truth were known, they were merely possessed by imaginary ideas about themselves.

I can be lifted and made to feel peaceful, or even get anxious or angry, all depending on what I listen to. What is it about music, old or new, that triggers such powerful emotions in a person?

For centuries, true music has been used in schools and monasteries to help seekers awaken. Music is vibration, so it is more readily taken in by the willing and receptive soul, and the vibrations themselves can be elevating, thereby temporarily altering the state of the listener. On the other hand, much of the music today sows the seed of either sentiment or conflict. To cancel any wrong state born in us through unconscious identification with certain of these vibratory states, we must learn how to watch ourselves while we listen to music. We must notice, consciously, its effect on ourselves.

This higher awareness will keep us awake to what the music is "making" of us.

> In terms of self-development, can you make a meaningful distinction between personal development and artistic development? It seems that the false self loves to invade even our best-intentioned artistic endeavors, i.e., nowhere are we more vulnerable to wanting the approval of others than where we are trying to somehow express ourselves artistically. Is there a meaningful way to stay connected to Real Life even when we must face our own artistic disappointments?

You are right—the line between inner development and artistic development can appear thin. But let me stress that it is appearance only. Ideally, the artist is working to express what has impressed itself upon his or her heart and mind. The joy in true creativity is the channeling of this energy into form while experiencing the formless nature that gave rise to it within us. Where we get into trouble, and not just in the arts, is when we are dragged into unconsciously deriving a sense of self from the visiting energy. Learn to make the distinction between the native and original creative impulse, and the attending sense of self that immediately floods in to take the credit. Most so-called artistic disappointments are just the flip side of first thinking ourselves special, and then, when conditions beyond our control affect our efforts, not living up to our own unconscious and inflated self-images.

> In those magical moments of clarity when my false self seems to have lost its hold on me and I feel God's presence, I start laughing at myself—at the pointlessness of all the worries that consumed me just moments before.

> I am happy just to be alive, and I can't stop grinning.
> Then I think to myself, "Uh-oh, if I'm this happy,
> something must be wrong." I'd like to escape this
> vicious circle.

The point of all true spiritual work is to place ourselves in relationship with the joy that is Real Life. Don't let doubt-filled thoughts rob you of those moments when you are rewarded for seeing through their hold on you. But by the same token, don't rob yourself of the chance to go higher still by seeing yourself (being ever watchful) as you enjoy these rewards. There is always something higher.

> Because of my inner work, I had this spiritual moment
> beyond description. I felt as though I was riding a wave
> of emotion that turned into an ocean of love. For a few
> days, I was as happy as any soul could have hoped to
> be. Then my bliss faded until I was just with me again.
> Now I want to go back! I keep asking why this hap-
> pened to me and how I can return to paradise, but I'm
> lost. Any insights you have here would be greatly
> appreciated.

As difficult or unwanted as this may sound, we have to let go of our memories of any higher states of oneness with God. If we don't, we only wind up pursuing an image; and pleasurable as those past pictures and corresponding feelings may be of what once came to us, they are in the way of our coming to the sanctuary of reality, where the oneness we seek is waiting for our entrance. Give up the painful questions like why this happened to you. The you that is asking is not the Real You at all. If you remember your glimpse, for practical purposes, the beauty of it was that there was no you within that moment as you presently feel yourself now.

Let the Love of Truth
Give You a Fearless Life

Science now knows what enlightened sages have been saying since time began: The true nature of all things is change. Everything is always *becoming*. Which means nothing can be truly considered without taking into account those forces driving these invisible changes.

What science has yet to learn is that these governing forces working behind all becoming possess their own intelligence, and that all things are transforming endlessly according to their relationship with this intelligence.

Creatures with fixed natures must become what their natures dictate. Lions, flowers, and fish are without choice in this respect. However, human beings are endowed with certain features in their nature that may allow them to choose what they become. And since the choice is not whether to become one thing or another, but rather in whose likeness we are becoming, the wise among us see this fact and work accordingly to align themselves with those forces intuited to be for the highest good. Then their goodness becomes our own, and our lives become their expression. Here is the key to this highest of relationships:

Learning to love what is good begins with being truthful about what we presently love and what we are becoming because of our relationship with it. This higher level of self-awareness actually transforms the life it becomes aware of, and as we are transformed by it—and begin becoming new within it—then we know the true benefit of being a lover of Truth is that this Love becomes us. And, as the following benefits are designed to reveal, this ever-renewing Love fears nothing!

- Only the lover of Truth knows the one Love that increases itself even as it waits patiently for him to expire all of his other loves.

- Only the lover of Truth knows that for every truth willingly endured arrives a greater willingness to endure even more—for she also knows that the harsh light she now sees herself in heralds not the end of her life, but holds its true beginning.

- Only the lover of Truth knows the unyielding attractive force of that truth not yet his own, and that beckons him to forsake all else for its dawning.

- Only the lover of Truth can know that singular fearlessness that comes with knowing there is no such thing as any truth to be feared.

- Only the lover of Truth recognizes the secret goodness hidden in the heart of every disappointment or sorrow.

- Only the lover of Truth has the wisdom not to condemn herself, or another, for any weakness revealed—for she knows that any truth revealed to the lover of Truth is the same as one already on its way to being healed by that same Love.

- Only the lover of Truth knows that whatever love he has been given to know is not his, but belongs to Truth alone.

- Only the lover of Truth accepts the responsibility that attends such a love, including being willing to forsake herself for its sake.

- Only the lover of Truth rests content with all—or the little—that he may have, for his contentment rests not within what he may or may not possess, but with his love of being the possession of the truth that he loves.

Pondering these truths about our relationship with Truth helps us to realize their promise of a fearless life. Here is a good way to put into practice these new ideas: Winning the Love in your heart that you know you want begins with awakening to what you now love without knowing it. Every day, every moment you can, come wide awake to yourself and see the false friends you have been holding near and dear within your heart. Don't judge . . . just see. Let the facts speak louder than the protests of what they reveal.

To begin seeing that negative states such as anger, impatience, worry, and fear have lodged themselves into the hidden corners of your heart is to discover how they have managed to win their spot. Now it is clear. These internal imposters were able to convince you that their embrace is the same as the strength, safety, and love for which you long. They are not. Bring their punishing presence in your heart into the light of your higher awareness—and your love of this awareness. Do this, and Love itself will not only banish these imposters but also empower you with the presence of a new and perfect fearlessness.

nine

Relationships: The Pathway and the Promise of Real Life

Hidden in the center of each human heart dwells a great spiritual secret. Left undiscovered, as it often remains for most of the masses, its presence causes the soul that harbors it to spend its days on earth seeking it knows not what, finding what is never enough, and then starting out all over again. But once this secret tells itself, the truth it reveals opens the heart that is its home, and leads the weary seeker to a whole new and higher relationship with life.

What is this great spiritual secret that we are created with, and that we must come to know if we are ever to end our wanderings and realize that peaceful strength we long for? *The relationship our heart longs for already exists.*

Yes, it is true; in spite of our unending sense that something is missing from our lives, the strange thing is that most of us already have had some experience with the truth of this great secret. We have felt its peaceful presence like a consoling whisper whenever we look up and witness an open-ended starry night or whenever good fortune lets us catch sunlight dancing on shaded leaves. And who hasn't felt the comfort that comes in taking silent notice of a mother loving away the fears of her small child?

In moments such as these we are touched—however briefly—by a life that somehow seems greater, more whole than our own. And in these precious, passing moments we are reminded there is something eternal, something ever green and good, as near to us as our own sensing of it. In this fulfilling instant, we are transported beyond ourselves and, all too briefly, find our aching heart and restless mind quieted. There is nothing to do, nowhere to go, no one who needs more than what this moment reveals. But because we don't yet understand the actual nature of this sublime moment— how it appears and from where it goes—it becomes the seed of our discontent. We then spend our days searching for ways either to relocate or otherwise re-create the heaven from which we feel we were unjustly cast. And as we all know too well, nothing we can do is enough; nowhere we know to turn leads us back to that peaceable kingdom. What we don't know is why this is so. Here is the reason: In our unconscious certainty of what we should be looking for, it hasn't yet dawned on us that we don't know where to look!

In a certain sense, living as we do in our state of spiritual sleep, we are not unlike a titled nobleman with extensive properties who—having fallen from his horse and striking his head—stumbles into a huntsmen's hut located on a distant part of his own property. Having now forgotten his real identity, he settles in and takes to believing that he must be the huntsman, and therefore he just assumes that small, gated yard in front of his hut must comprise the extent and range of his holdings. And just as we might assume this nobleman would feel a sense of limitation created by his accidental circumstances, so do we feel the constraint of our own captive consciousness. The sole purpose of truth teachings is to reveal and release us from these self-imposed restrictions. Follow the next few special insights to freedom:

In those more contented times when, for the moment, we are at rest with who we are because our gaze has fallen upon a secret corner of some world bright and brimming, *we have not peeked into a place residing outside us.* Not at all. The reason we see that timelessness in the night sky, or feel that fleeting brush with the gentle touch of goodness, is because we have just looked into and touched a small corner of the unknown universe of our Self. This revelation can be summarized by saying that *we are what we see,* and that our brief bliss in these magical moments is the reward of coming into relationship with Real Life. St. Francis, the illuminative wise man and Christian mystic, intones the truth of this same important self-discovery:

> I never think upon eternity without receiving great comfort. For I say to myself: How could my soul grasp the idea of everlastingness, if the two were not related in some way?

What this saint tells us is that right within us, as an unseen aspect of our True Nature, resides the entire range of relationships that the universe has to offer. Think of it! But through the eyes of our present understanding, each time conditions grant us this fleeting sense of a brighter, broader order of existence, we attribute these expansive feelings to our participation in an event greater than ourselves. This perception is one supported by the sense-supplied "fact" that this moment is the effect of an event taking place "outside" of ourselves.

But our actual experience in these moments *is not outside of us*. The better explanation of these brief illuminations is that we, ourselves, have been momentarily transported outside the limited range of an unconscious set of internal relationships. The best way to explain this new idea is to paint a picture we can all recognize.

We all know that when we really *see* a breathtaking sunset, we *feel* it; we take part in its vibrant colors. But we couldn't possibly share in this beauty *before* us if the essence of this painted sky above us wasn't *within* us. In other words, the depth of this beauty—and the inner delight it elicits—are actually aspects of our own consciousness. If we can begin to see the truth of this discovery, then we are prepared for our next step in how to realize Real Life through relationships.

The world of people and events we see spinning "around" us is, in reality, a kind of special mirror. This interesting idea helps shed light on why all of the great and timeless world philosophies have called the world an illusion. What is the purpose of this mirroring world? It is to show us . . . *us*! Which brings us to another key point of this study.

As we realize the truth of ourselves, that who we *really* are (including all that we can come to know about ourselves) *already exists* in this one great relationship from which we are never apart, so do we realize Real Life. Let's examine this important finding using our personal experience to prove its validity.

More than simply identifying, we've all seen that it's possible to suddenly "know" what a child feels opening up a gift, and how in these moments our pleasure is as good as his own. Most of us have been surprised to find ourselves "knowing" (beyond mere anthropomorphism) what's going on in the mind of our dog or cat, and what a kind of delight there is in sharing these unique sensations. The point is that we can't take something into ourselves that doesn't already have a counterpart in our consciousness, else how would we recognize this quality, let alone savor it?

We are now very near being able to see, for the first time, the real stumbling block before us in our search for happiness and contentment. Allow all that we have discovered to bring its light to bear on these next few ideas. Our sense of self-limitation, of feeling ourselves incomplete, is not a result of our relationships with the world revolving *around* us. The real problem is that we have been living from an unconscious part of ourselves *incapable of relating* to anything outside the limited range of its own conditioned content. The following explanation should not only serve to bring this last inclusive insight to life, but reveal, by its light, how we can begin using all of our relationships to realize Real Life.

In days long past, seekers of Truth spoke of a mysterious "lost chord." Perhaps you are familiar with this timeless spiritual idea? Roughly speaking, the search for this lost chord centered on an idea not too dissimilar from the one that drove seekers to try to find the legendary philosopher's stone. If someone could discover, group, and then intone certain musical notes together—at the right time and in the right setting—the sound of this celestial chord created by certain planetary tones would elevate that person's consciousness.

Just as it was then, and is today (with all forms of scripture), instead of realizing that this idea represented an internal process, people made this spiritual principle a literal, physical quest. But the real meaning (which can't be stated, only realized) in this idea of a lost chord might be spoken thus: Each of us is created as a special kind of instrument whose purpose is threefold—to "sing" the notes of the celestial universe, to act as a soundboard for other songs and, in this resonance, in this relationship with the reality of life, to *know* Real Life.

Imagine for a moment that a young child, whom we will name Christine, is given a harplike instrument on her birthday. Further, that in her first few days of playing with it, maybe due to her reach or hand size, she is able to stroke and sound out only five of the harp's one hundred and eight strings. Now let's say that Christine grows increasingly identified with just the tones of these five strings and decides, accordingly, to play only them in their various configurations. With this image in mind, see how the following outcome would be an inevitable one for Christine, giving her an almost constant but undetected sense that something is missing from her life.

Each time Christine plays the five strings she perceives as being the harp's entire worthwhile range, she also hears—though barely audible—the instrument's remaining, unsounded strings. Why is this true? It is a universal law that they must vibrate in sympathetic tones. Sometimes their resonance delights her. Other times, depending on the grouping of the strings she plays, their tones trouble her in their dissonance. And that's not all!

Then there are those days when Christine's friends come to visit, bringing with them their instruments. More than likely, because of the world in which they live and the ideas with which they have been inculcated, each of her friends has chosen a slightly different set of three to five strings to play. Some of the tones struck by her visiting friends naturally harmonize with the ones Christine plays and enjoys, while others strike an immediate discord. It's no wonder why each child goes back and forth between praising and blaming the music of each other's instrument for being the cause of how they feel. We could keep going with this illustration, but the point is already well made.

We are *all* notes. We are all the notes of the Kingdom. We have proven this by revealing how each of us is able to resonate with things we would never dream could produce either such a soothing or scary resonance in us. What should be evident in this fact is that when the "sound," or manifestation, of someone else sets us off and sends us into a fit, it is not their vibration that vexes us and makes us a "victim." What really disturbs us is the internal vibrations of a few of our own unknown strings as they sound off (within us) in a natural sympathetic response to the dominating tones of the moment.

Our recurring resistance to these undesired moments, to such people and conditions as create in us this discord we mistakenly blame on them, keeps us from learning how to utilize these relationships in order to realize their true purpose for us. For instance, say there is someone at work who tends to irritate us. Our usual approach is to avoid this person, as our errant thinking tells us that being out of sight is out of mind. The only thing is, as we have all come to experience, we cannot escape the sound of our self; so if it isn't that person we dodge at work, surely someone else will come along and strike a similar chord, "making" us hear those same sorry sounds of self again.

What is the answer? To realize deeply, personally, that we cannot outrun any one of these sounds of ourselves anymore than a piano can move out from under the strings by which it plays; and, as an integral part of this new self-understanding, that we need not, *must not,* resist some unpleasant note of our own, or that of someone else. These notes, whatever their tone, do not define us unless we make the mistake of identifying with their sounding. The false sense of self that each such sound produces within us is just that: a temporary self that is, itself, little more than a passing effect of the blending of these sounding notes.

To change our relationship with life, to realize its unlimited song, we must bravely learn what it means to hear *all* of ourselves. Here is the key to this new relationship: Our quiet awareness of any one sound of ourselves, regardless of its bright or dark tone, is the field of relationship and not its sole content. What does this mean? When we see a spring pasture, our pleasure is derived from seeing the whole of it— all of its colors, each of its shapes. Imagine judging a field of flowers by picking out one weed.

As we learn how to listen to the sounds of life within ourselves, as we open up to life's endless relationships by becoming aware of them within ourselves without limiting their sounds simply because they don't agree with our present five-note self, *then* we begin to realize our Real Life. We hear at last within ourselves the lost chord that has always been our True Self.

Gaining Uncommon Insights from Our Everyday Interactions

I have frequent struggles to be myself around others, especially when I feel someone is superior to me. What can I do to help regain myself in this situation?

Try to see the difference between what you actually are in the moment (around others) versus what thoughts and feelings are telling you that you ought to be. As this grows clearer, through your practice of placing mindfulness before self-protection, you will begin to taste that the fear you feel trying to protect you is what you are trying to protect yourself from.

When speaking to a group of people, I often experience a feeling that I am just acting, and sometimes even lose my train of thought because it all seems a bit silly. Would you please comment on this?

Your experience is a certain level of awakening to yourself. What is happening is that there now is a part of you present enough to observe the flow of personality. Personality is an actor. As you keep growing, you will be able to watch this actor with the confidence of being the director of its actions, knowing that it can do only what you allow it to do. Don't let your findings disturb you.

Being around groups of people seems to put me into some kind of negative trance. I become an uptight collection of ego, shame, anger, and fear that forgets everything I have learned. Would you please address the issue of what I can do at work or around groups of people that might help?

Your comment shows you are beginning to come awake to yourself. Stay in the middle of the battle. It is never the people we are around that cause us to experience negative reactions. These reactions arise out of what we secretly want from people. As your inner conflict becomes increasingly conscious to you, you will have to choose whether or not to continue being "you" or to give yourself up in order to learn the lessons in these relationships, inner and outer, that await you.

When I manage to remember my higher aim in life, I seem to lose control of my life, and other people are quick to take advantage of what they evidently see as my weakness. Should this be happening or am I going about something all wrong?

This may sound strange at first, but let anyone who wants to take advantage of your wish to awaken take whatever they will. This doesn't mean to turn your money or property, etc., over to sharks. But it does mean not to be afraid of letting everyone in the world see what you think they think is your weakness. The issue has nothing to do with others, but with our perception of ourselves. *Dare to be no one.* Only when you realize that you already are no one (and yet more than you know) will the fear of others taking advantage of you disappear. After all, what can anyone else take from you? God has seen to it that everyone everywhere receives the reward of his own nature moment to moment to moment. What this means is that anyone who wishes to harm you has first harmed himself. And believe me, you can't make it any tougher on this person than he has already made it on himself.

How do we recognize and accept our responsibility to others? Is there any compromise or sacrifice to self when fulfilling our responsibility to others—especially our family?

If you have a responsibility, fulfill it. You must take care of your children. If you have a sick parent, and there is no one else to help them, you should be a good son or daughter. If, on the other hand, you have a twenty-five-year-old child living at home that you can't say "no" to, this is a completely different story. We must each find out where it is that we accept a life of fear, calling it a necessary compromise, and, on the other hand, how it can be equally true that we won't compromise with others out of some self-image or other fear. So, what do you really want? Truth does not deny anyone its Life based on what responsibilities that person may have. In fact, quite the opposite is true. It is the person who refuses real responsibility that the Truth doesn't see.

Dealing with the Darkness We Get from Others

In relationships, why does it seem as though it's the honest people in life who are forever being lied to? Does evil win this way, or what?

Would you like to hear a timeless truth that most of us have either forgotten we already know or that is sadly discounted today because of the prevailing sick socioeconomic conditions? *Honesty is its own reward.* We receive, moment to moment, the "reward" of our own nature. Let the liars lie. You be true. That is all you have to know and do. Don't be concerned with the liar's fate; it is sealed with every lie told.

Why do I feel let down when I ask for help in doing a task and see that a family member is not concerned with the request? If they were doing the asking, the situation would be different—that is, they would be upset if I didn't help them!

One of the major stumbling blocks as we go further with our spiritual studies is the gradual discovery of the undeveloped nature of the human beings around us. It never occurs to us how truly self-centered others are, and when we begin to see this, the observation brings a sense of despair or of being alone. This is inevitable and valuable to your work—the reason being that as we see through the secret self-interest that possesses our friends and family, we can't help but come aware of it within ourselves. This does two things: First, we begin to become truly self-reliant, and second, at the same time as we learn to let go of our own selfishness, we understand its mechanical and unconscious nature in others. This teaches us compassion.

In my job I must deal daily with a few dozen emotionally dark coworkers. I can tolerate just so many of these kinds of people per day (as we all have to), but a few dozen is just too many for me to take. What can I do to handle this situation better, besides getting another job?

I know that it is difficult to be surrounded by toxic people; however, as difficult as this is to understand, your present work circumstance is perfect for your continuing development, if you understand how to use it. I say "how to use it" because as long as you don't, wherever you go, you will continue to encounter "hateful" people, and your own negative reaction will use you up. Try this: Determine that when you walk in the door, your attention will remain with your reactions to these people and not on the people themselves. This shift in your attention will help you realize what it is you really need to be free of . . . namely, "you"! And "need" is the key word in this instance. You'll see, if you'll practice this approach, that it is just "you" jumping all over "you." Once this is clear, then you can jump out of "you."

Without reverting to their lower level, how do you get people to stop making hurtful, cut-down remarks?
One of the reasons people pounce on or attack us the way they do is that they are feeding off of us in many different ways, especially when we return a negative energy. For an amazing experience, try sometime consciously refusing your own negativity in the face of someone else's. Just go silent, and then watch what happens to the person who attacked you. The odds are, you will watch this person have a change of heart right in the middle of their attack. And even if they don't change their behavior, your new behavior will leave you feeling better about yourself.

In a world where people seem to become increasingly more rude every day, how does one cope and act or react when people seem to be so cold and basically indifferent to each other?

One of the important aspects of this work is beginning to employ its principles in our everyday lives. What does this mean? Any condition we meet that is unwanted, such as a rude person, is not the cause of our stress. All conditions simply offer a momentary mirror for us in which it is possible to begin seeing what we have brought with us, within ourselves, into that moment. There is no sense in trying to change people without first changing the part of ourselves that believes our very sense of self, of well-being, somehow depends on how others treat us. Step back from your own reactions. Don't give them your life, and you'll discover they have a life of their own . . . and that you want nothing to do with it.

The Reality Behind the Need for Realizing New Relationships

Most of my friends feel I have gone off the deep end, and I have noticed a growing separation between us as I work more and more for my own spiritual freedom. It is not that I don't care for them, but rather I am becoming less and less concerned about the things that have always driven all of us. My fear is they will eventually want to have nothing to do with me. Is it normal for friendships to pass as people change their life and level? Is this what Christ meant when he said "Let the dead bury their dead"?

Yes, quite often old friends will fall away as you work on changing your interior relationship and begin seeing more about this life and its true purpose. Think of the company that a caterpillar keeps and then, as it is transformed, how its new friends have wings and inhabit the sky. Letting go of those who want to remain earthbound is at least in part the true inner meaning of this passage of Christ's that you have cited.

> Because I see it as counterproductive to my spiritual work, I have recently stopped sharing my negative states with a person near and dear to me, a friend who is also a practicing psychotherapist. Now he seems threatened by this new action on my part. He sees "sharing one's feelings" as the way to achieve and maintain intimacy. I don't feel that I can go back to the relationship the way it was. Can you comment on this?

Congratulations! Through your inner work, you have stumbled onto a great discovery. Your sensing and understanding of this change in relationship is accurate. This person needs to feed on your weaknesses in order to feel strong. By your refusing to supply the food (of negative concerns), the creature feeding suddenly shows itself. Don't be afraid to see all of this and its implications. The change that must occur as a result of your choice not to be in a conspiracy of woes will be the dawning of a new and higher consciousness within yourself.

> How do we find others who are also searching for their true selves? At times the search causes us to leave former friends behind—not because we are better, but because we are different.

Here is a highly encouraging thought: The study of Truth leads us to those relationships that are beneficial to the Truth we are studying. It could be said that as you grow in your love of Truth/God, your newly emerging nature is a law unto itself that naturally repels what is dissimilar to it and likewise attracts what is helpful, healthy, and loving. In short, while it is good to find others who are interested in the Truth as a part of our own free will, the search for others who are embracing their true nature is ultimately directed by our own wish for the Truth.

I am having trouble understanding how to leave my relationships with friends and family alone. It seems that the changes I feel are affecting them, but neither they nor I understand some of these changes. It is an extremely confusing time for everyone in my life. Can you help me ease this effect?

The Truth asks us to give it its way in our lives. The relationships established before the dawning of any such light within us are naturally going to be put through necessary changes by the inclusion of this new understanding as it dawns within us. Try to understand that we live in a world of which we see only a tiny, tiny part. But even in those small glimpses of our physical reality can we see hints of the celestial one. What happens to the creatures living in any environment when that environment is changed? Some naturally stay, some must leave, and most importantly, as it concerns our work, new creatures are attracted. Continue with your work. Be willing to let the chips fall where they may with all of your relationships. Be kind, but above all, be true. The rest will take care of itself.

Using Your Relationships
to Realize Real Life

The greatest, most abundant resource on planet Earth is also its least understood and utilized. Its unlimited supply is found virtually everywhere, anytime, and under all circumstances, even though few recognize its real value. What is this most precious collective resource? It is our *relationships*.

Consider these truths: It is within relationships that we grow as individuals in everything valuable, because it is *through* them that we become stronger and wiser, allowing us to realize a love that transcends our unseen self-limiting self-interests. Yet, even though we may acknowledge the existence of this path to self-perfection, the essential mystery of exactly *how* to use this endless resource remains obscured.

What do we have to do to change the balance sheet of our lives so that for every measure of impatience and intolerance there may be at least an equivalent sum of compassion and consideration? How do we learn to use our relationships with others to realize a new kind of relationship with ourselves wherein we are able to discover that who we *really* are is all we need to be?

Your willingness to work your way through the twelve special practices of the following inner exercise—to strive to employ these higher ideals in your relationships with others—will reward you with the Real Life your heart longs for. The main thrust of these special practices is to show you how to use each developing moment in your relationships with family, friends, and coworkers to consciously change your relationship with yourself. Only a moment's consideration will show us the wisdom of this unusual inner work.

With few exceptions, the usual focus of our attention and interactions with others is centered on our self and the fulfillment of its desires. "How do *I* feel about you?" "What do *I* want from him?" or "When will she realize that *I* know best?" In other words, the mindset of the false self, under most circumstances, is "Me first." By forever placing its own considerations before considering any other, it remains the master of its own universe, even if all that revolves through it is its own imagined importance.

The great inner life lesson to be learned in working with the following twelve suggested practices is that what we put first in our lives *is our first relationship with life*. And it is *this* relationship that secretly determines the nature of all others in our lives. Through our willingness to work at placing our usual self in "second place," we agree not only to change the way we see our relationships, but we have also agreed to be changed by the truths our new relationships will inevitably show us about us.

- Be as alert to what you can do to help someone else in any given moment as you are critically aware of others for failing to notice your immediate needs.

- Let anyone who wants to psychologically defeat you have his victory, and do it without revealing that you chose to give him the last word.

- In any moment of consequence, be as willing to see that you may be wrong as you are convinced that you are always right.

- Do whatever act of kindness you may be moved to do for another person without drawing attention to your deed, or to yourself for having done it.

- Look for ways to make moments work to the advantage of someone else besides yourself.

- When gathered with friends or family, instead of competing for the spotlight, voluntarily help to shine it on someone whom you know its light will emotionally lift or otherwise encourage.

- Even when you know that you are solidly in the right, rather than rub it in, sacrifice your righteousness.

- Should a sarcastic or unkind remark pop into your mind to tease, torment, or in any way "trash" another person, try swallowing it first to see how it tastes before you dish it out.

- Whatever it might be when your "moment in the sun" arises—such as being acknowledged or applauded for a deed well done—if you have the choice, give the best or better portion away.

- Let there be times when you don't tell someone everything you know about her problem, even if your understanding of it is better than hers.

- When feeling displeased with someone, don't show your displeasure, and save any necessary correction for a later time.

- There are times when the greatest strength (and kindness) one can possess is to allow another his weakness without pointing it out or otherwise punishing him for it.

Just a few last thoughts about this exercise to take with you: Remember that all spiritual practices are a means to self-discovery, and that discouragement, or any form of frustration, are secret indicators of some end we have in mind that has been thwarted. Lastly, keep in mind that everything true we discover about ourselves enlarges our relationship with life, and that there is no end to these relationships . . . just as Real Life is endless.

ten

Helping Others to Help Themselves Go Higher

While the range of human crises runs the gamut of experience, few would argue that the most difficult of these trials always involves some form of an unwanted change in one of our relationships. We know them all too well. From events as divergent as reaching a crossroads with a close friend where you must each now go your own way, to being left by someone who no longer loves you, right up and through those complex personal challenges such as dealing with being betrayed or the news of a loved one's impending demise . . . all are difficult, each causes upheaval, and none is wanted.

And yet . . . what if we could find within these challenging moments of our relationships a common thread, a single truth woven throughout them that reveals a secret purpose to their existence? And further, what if we could uncover within this unseen purpose a plan to help us fulfill the purpose of our own lives? Wouldn't such a discovery change the way in which we look at everything? Of course it would. So, let's begin this study by first looking at the "end" of any one of our own relationship crises: that moment when the tempest finally passes and we know our heart and mind have been tempered to a new strength. Parts of our self have been thrown out—forced out, in some instances. Old aspects of our self have merged into new essences that emerge with new desires. In this strange and mixed aftermath we stand upon the fertile ground of a whole new understanding about life. But there is more.

Within us, pushing its way to the forefront of our consciousness, we sense the arrival of a newly born yet higher order of self-knowledge. In other words, we emerge from the passing of this relationship-based crisis a remade creature. There is little doubt of this. It is a stronger, wiser person that exits these relationships than the one who enters into them.

The point made here surely reveals one of the main purposes of these personal trials. Through them *we are made to grow.* This is an idea that we will see has two meanings: First, in the sense of our being created to develop and grow within ourselves through our relationships; and second, that we must go through certain kinds of continual changes *with others* in order to realize this spiritual growth. This much we can see as true. But if our individual growth is somehow interdependent with our relationships, then implied in these discoveries is one last truth to be revealed.

There is a unique and unseen relationship between our own spiritual development and helping others to realize the new levels of self-understanding necessary for their inner growth. With this insight in mind, it is vital not to discount the following just because its information seems so obvious at first telling, for hidden within these commonly known facts of life are hints about fulfilling our celestial destiny.

For us to grow into anything—as does a child who discards one pair of shoes for the next size larger, or the adult who abandons his former way of thinking in favor of a higher, healthier level of self-understanding—requires first that *we outgrow an existing body of restraints.* Physically speaking, this process of law is easy to grasp. We grow into the need for new clothes as we outgrow our former ones. We can't stop this natural bodily process.

On the other hand, our inner growth, our continuing spiritual development, is another story. Just as in the Old Testament story of Lot and his wife, who were told to climb to higher ground to escape the coming destruction of their decadent city, so we are required to leave behind us the lower levels of ourselves if we wish to reach a higher inner ground. Again, this much may be obvious as it concerns our individual spiritual growth, but what do these findings have to do with helping others to help themselves go higher?

One of the principal ways we can help others to achieve new inner growth *is by outgrowing ourselves.* To help us understand the wisdom in this new idea we must first consider another equally important idea. A great portion of the way we "see" ourselves—images of ourselves from which we derive our sense of self—is actually a provision of our relationships with friends and family. Consider, for instance, that much of the way we measure the value of ourselves is secretly connected to those values we attribute to others close to us. For real-life examples of this pivotal idea we need only look into any close relationship of ours, but for now I'll draw upon the relationship I share with my wife in order to illustrate this particular point.

However I may look upon myself (perhaps as being kind, strong, or whatever the self-picture may be), this self-image is very much connected with an image of my wife that I hold in my mind's eye as being loving and wise herself. After all, I wouldn't take much stock in seeing myself as being worthwhile in her eyes (or those of any other person, for that matter) if I didn't believe that she was worthwhile, too. But the "danger" here—in this largely unconscious, complex set of relationships shared with those closest to us—becomes painfully obvious the moment one of these persons exhibits behavior "unbecoming" of them *according to our* vested idea of what makes them valuable to us. For in this same instant we perceive them as having shifted even slightly right or left of *our* designated center (for them), it is *we* who suddenly find ourselves feeling unsettled, angry, or strangely fearful.

At some point in our lives we have all dealt with uncomfortable moments where an unexpected or unwanted change in one near to us brings up some unpleasant reaction in us. Of course we are usually very quick to find fault with this person, but here is the real, invisible story. The reason we fall under the rule of these reaction-driven dark states, and then find ourselves trying to dictate the life direction of the "offending" person, is that something within us feels thrown for a loss. To understand why this is true, consider as deeply as possible the following insight, for it holds special clues as to how we can outgrow our own painful condition as well as how we can help others to go higher.

The instant we perceive someone stepping outside "the box" of who we have always known them to be is the same moment in which we begin to fear the loss of who we need them to be in order to maintain our familiar sense of self. And, if we are honest with ourselves, this is the same moment in which we attempt, one way or another—either through promises or pressures—to get them back into the box.

In other words—and please keep in mind that our controlling behavior is unconscious to us, as no conscious person would inhibit the growth of another's being—something in us does not want this person to change. There is a sensing it will cost us too much—a great "personal" cost that we will cover in just a moment. The unconscious self that sleeps in us can intuit that allowing such a transformation to take place will demand a similar transformation within us. And the truth be known, this same false nature wants nothing to change other than the deepening crystallization of its own imagined greatness . . . a greatness that includes its outrageous image of how accepting it is of changes in life and in others!

These findings all point to one key idea. There is one essential ingredient missing in most of our relationships— one that is definitely required if we wish to continue in our own development and help others to do the same. What is this powerful catalyst that only we can provide for each other? *Room in which to grow.*

We can help others reach higher by simply agreeing, consciously, to give them space to go through their changes even when these changes may challenge our sense of self and its well-being. As just one simple example of how to help in this way, we must each learn to *keep ourselves quiet* when the actions of someone close to us start to disturb us. Why is this new kind of self-silence so important for the growth of both parties involved?

To begin with, the disturbance that we feel in these moments is caused by a tremor in us. This is to say that our shaky sense of self is an effect of some picture we have held of this person as it hits the ground and shatters. Apart from our children, whom we must guide through their developing years, we need to learn to leave people alone with their decisions and corresponding actions. There is already a truth, a wisdom that supports this conscious course of action.

We already understand that no action of ours ever goes without its commensurate reward. This eternal principle is best known as karma, the great, inescapable law of cause and effect. This means it is our own nature—as the backstage parent of what prods us along in life—that determines what we experience as our life. So too is it with our family and friends; each receives what he or she is—no more, no less. This truth tells us why we must not only give them room to make the choices that they will, but then leave them alone to realize and experience the unique results of being who they are. How else can they learn and grow beyond themselves?

Understanding these truths mandates that we back off from being secretly on everyone's back, that we give them the inner room they need to grow and discover themselves.

The difficulty here is that in order to give others this space they need, we must first make room within ourselves. To state this same idea differently, we must remove ourselves from our habitual inner places of judgments, opinions, and knowing better than anyone else. We have always called this place that must be left behind our "self."

This conscious sacrifice of self—of who we conceive ourselves to be for the sake of who our friend or loved one is yet to be—gives new meaning to the beautiful ideal of "laying our life down for our brother." This is how we help others to help themselves go higher . . . by daring to grow beyond ourselves.

Escape the Punishment in Judging Others

I know that when I look at people, I end up judging them on superficial things. I also know that this hurts my relationships as well as myself. I want to stop. How do I turn this judgmental nature off whenever I see something in someone that doesn't meet my approval?

The idea is not to try to turn off this nature, but to come awake to the actual experience of yourself that you have in these moments. Resisting thought does nothing. Learning to "taste" what judgmental thoughts bring to your inner table will teach you to leave the establishment called yourself.

It seems to me that we are always looking for faults and weaknesses in others . . . are we just covering up inferior feelings within ourselves?

By and large, everything we condemn in others is just a way of hiding something similar within ourselves.

Sometimes when I see people that seem—at least on the surface—not quite "all there," certain fears go through me, especially if I have to interact with these people. Why the fear?

This takes a little extra thought on your part, but it will be well worthwhile. Reactions of a negative nature that come up in us toward any human being arise out of the content of our own conditioned past. This conditioned nature fears anything within which it is not able to easily recognize itself, therefore it will judge or condemn anything it gazes upon, whether up close or at a distance. This state of self lives in an undetected state of fear because it is forever looking for itself, and when it doesn't immediately find this, it pushes away the offending object.

It seems that all I am seeing of late are the negative things in people and how much suffering this causes. I am not very comfortable with this development in myself, as I usually like to stress the positive. Will I get past this stage, or do I just have the wrong point of view?

One of the wonders of this Work is to begin experiencing the inner nature of the people around you. Don't avoid this, or think it misplaced. Gradually, as you become more inwardly sensitive to the manifestations of people, compassion is born. This higher inner awareness grants you patience and new forms of consideration, because now you realize just how much pain everyone is really in. Keep going.

The more I think I know about true spirituality, the more I become easily aggravated by the behavior of

others. I will be in a conversation, or overhearing a conversation, and hear someone make an obviously false (spiritually) statement, or I observe inconsistent behavior. I sense that part of my anger is seeing the inconsistency and false behavior in myself. What is the right way for me to handle these moments?

Stay with yourself. Don't put yourself into what you observe. It doesn't matter what anyone anywhere is doing or saying relative to your potential for inner development. The expression "The buck stops here" is valuable as long as we understand it to mean that these recurring blasts of unconscious energy we experience in moments such as these are to remain conscious within ourselves. We must not attribute their cause to someone or anything else outside of us. When we work with this truth and its instruction, then we begin to die to the blame-casting nature.

Giving and Receiving Spiritual Corrections

I know someone who drives me crazy, and I want to help him by sharing the truths I am learning. Without using interfering tactics, how can we help others to come awake to themselves?

One of the most difficult aspects of our work is learning to bear the unpleasant manifestations of people around us. But this can also help us grow quickly. If by interfering tactics you mean "make someone see the light," it is impossible. But if we will do our work, which often requires waiting out our own unpleasantness before speaking, then not only can we lend someone a helpful word or action, but they will see that we are behaving differently. This willingness on our part to inwardly accept the weight of our own burdens first is really the best invitation to others to become interested in this Work.

> **I see a great opportunity arising soon to speak the truth to someone about something, but I am deathly afraid to do so! Where can I find the courage I need to proceed?**

If you can see the truth of the following insight, it will lend you a surprising form of strength: Refusing any life-lessons increases their density. Besides which, there is no escaping the lessons that life would have us learn. Don't think about the outcome of being truthful; consider instead the effects of living with lies. Then, come awake and proceed!

> **If we know ahead of time that the right action is going to cause someone to suffer because of his or her falseness, that doesn't mean we shouldn't take the action, does it? If that is the case, what is the limit to inducing suffering to others?**

Whenever a right action presents itself to be taken, it should be taken. But let's be careful for a moment about "right action." One good way to know if your action is a right one as it concerns "straightening out" someone else is what you feel if you don't take that action. This is sensitive ground. One must be careful. Sometimes we must say certain corrective things to others. But one especially valuable inner practice is to wait for some period of time before expressing our view. This pause allows whomever takes it the chance to inwardly taste the nature that wants to make the correction.

If there is pressure to correct someone, you can be fairly certain your correction is not a right one, even if the words spoken are true. On the other hand, some of the best moments to point out confusion in others is when you are the most afraid to do so. Then the odds are that not only is your action right, but that person is likely to benefit from it as well.

I have great trouble dealing with friends and loved ones who ask me how I am doing with "the Lord"— especially when they then commence to teach me the error of my ways! How can I better deal with these moments other than by just getting mad?

We must each learn what it means to "lay down our lives for our brothers." The inner meaning of this is that it takes great interior patience, understanding, and eventually compassion to bear the unpleasant and often arrogant manifestations of people around us who, asleep in their unconscious righteousness, believe they are doing what is right. In this instance, you can use these individuals and any such encounters as a "spiritual springboard." What does this mean? Use your irritation to come awake to yourself. Consider the beam in your eye. Leave the others alone. If you'll try this, you'll begin to break free from the wrong parts of yourself that make you feel righteous in judging others. They will never know the sacrifice you are making, but you will, and freedom follows.

It is difficult to accept correction from other people. How do we judge the quality of correction when someone offers advice or criticism? I look at the unhappy lives of many of the people giving input, and think that

> their advice isn't worth much if they have such difficulties. On the other hand, I might be missing some valuable correction. Any advice?

Do you remember the old expression "If the shoe fits, wear it"? Well, in our spiritual work, any reaction we have to a correction proves that our shoes not only fit, but they are laced too tight. We can use everything that is thrown at us (right or wrong) to walk away from what is wrong within ourselves. This path naturally turns every so-called "wrong" into a right.

Guidance That Helps Your Loved Ones Grow

> **What steps can one take to point young children in their right path so they won't have to face so many problems growing up?**

Children and sponges have a lot in common. They soak up what is around them. Words that are in contrast with conditions are soaked up by children in the form of conflict. Our task is first to learn how to learn ourselves. As we actually begin learning, our very nature becomes our teacher. This is the best we can do for children until they are old enough to begin connecting their aches and pains with the choices made by their "intelligence."

> **How can we parents, who are just beginning to obtain the least bit of understanding of the truth, best instill in our children the will to seek and understand the truth for themselves?**

It is better for your children to see you struggle and fail at what is real than to try to convince them that they should pretend to be true. We live in a world that is far greater in its invisible influences than what we experience with our eyes and ears. This means that any real effort to put the truth first with your children means that they will experience your wish and receive the right encouragement from your attempts. We must all increasingly learn to stop believing in pictures we have of ourselves and opt for what reality reveals to us. This is our healing . . . and eventually, everyone else's.

Is it possible to use my marriage to further my studies in self-development? If so, how?

The whole of our lives is relationship. The whole of our inner discovery takes place within relationship. What this means is that regardless of the place of relationship (i.e., marriage, family, work), here is where we need to work. Nothing can speed up our inner work better than working with someone who makes us see the need for change. The closer the relationship, the more likely this dynamic exists. On the other hand, your spiritual work does not depend upon the compliance of anyone else. Your wish to work inwardly cannot be impeded by any other human being. The beauty in this is that as you grow, you automatically provide space for those around you to realize that a higher possibility exists. If these people are at all sensitive, they will be drawn to you and want to know what you are about. If not, Truth will take the matter into its own hands and resolve the issues.

I know I should not worry about certain things in life; however, what am I to do when loved ones have chosen things that are not in keeping with the things that they have learned? What can I do to keep them safe and to guide them back on the right road?

Inner work is not about trying not to worry. It is about seeing that worry doesn't work. How can a person who gives away his or her own life to every passing negative state (regardless of its seeming cause) hope to guide someone else? If you want to help another, free yourself, or at least make that your sole intention. From this work, and its upward-trending results, you will have new answers to help yourself and your loved ones.

> I find I want to share the truths I learn with friends and relatives, especially a relative of mine who is going through a divorce and is on the verge of suicide. Will it be counterproductive to share with her? Should I keep my information to myself and just listen? I find I am pushing people away at times.

This is one of those lessons that is only learned in the schoolroom of personal experience. You know the saying "Cast not your pearls . . ." and yet, if you sense in anyone around you a receptivity to what is true, and more importantly, a need for it, then it is your right responsibility to pass along the Truth as best you can. Here is a hint: Don't try to teach others, but rather let what you love about these teachings speak for you to them.

The Work of Bringing Light into the World

> Is there a way we can know we are ready to teach others? I have tried and found I normally make things worse. How do I find the balance between the urge to help and when to be quiet?

It is the essence of our lives that determines the relationships we have with others. Teaching is a lot simpler than we imagine. For instance, what do we teach others when we are angry or anxious? What do we teach others when they see us afraid of some news? This is one level of teaching. On the other hand, there are natural times when (and this is important to note) someone you know will actually ask you for some insight or help. Then not only is it natural, but necessary, that you give what "water" you can to ease their thirst. Under no circumstances should you try to teach others anything they haven't asked for. This kind of teaching comes from the wrong parts of ourselves and is a secret act of aggression and arrogance. Learn to taste the difference. The Truth will take care of the rest.

Should we try to help someone with their spiritual development, or must they be receptive? What mistake can there be in presenting a few truths to others with the hope that the ideas strike a right chord within them?

There are laws that govern all things, including our own development as well as that of others. Sometimes the most difficult, yet most true, thing we can do in the moment is to let others learn what is true for themselves. Sometimes we attempt to "help others" because we are unconsciously trying to change them according to our own ideas of what they should be like. When we do this, it not only creates resistance in the person we address, but it keeps us asleep to our own interior and misguided ambitions. We must all learn to be awake around others so that we can learn to feel whether or not what that person asks is arising from a genuine wish to know.

What is the best way to respond to people who inquire about the esoteric books I read (yours and others)? My experience in responding to these questions has not been very positive.

Your experience is something all of us have shared when it comes to trying to discuss higher matters with others that seem to want to know what we are up to. Try to stay awake in these kinds of encounters. Rely upon your intuition to tell you whether or not these people are sincerely interested in esoteric studies, or are just looking for something to occupy their time with by stealing yours. As a matter of fact, it is good work to refuse to give argumentative types what they are looking for . . . and if you'll do this, they will reveal the nature that engaged you. This is the best teacher of all. Plus, your refusal to fall into their world tells them a lot if they have eyes to see what you can do. If they can't see this, then there is nothing that could be said anyway. Let these people go, and continue with your wish to become a new human being.

With all the demands on my time in day-to-day life, I find it difficult to do much beyond what meets the needs of my family. How crucial is it that I dedicate some time to helping spread the truth to other people? And how can I do that without seeming like some kind of missionary?

It is so important that we do our correct part to help spread the light, but this need not be a big thing. And as long as we remain considerate of others, and what may be their wish to be left alone, how we do our work can be as simple as the following: Maybe make an effort to elevate the table talk at a meal to include a right idea you heard or are interested in, or don't pick up a negative comment someone throws at you. The point is to be active in putting the truth first. Everything you do to help or encourage someone else along the way strengthens and encourages both of you. Of this there is no doubt. All things good come to those for whom the good is all things.

In conversations with others, I find myself insisting on being "right." Why should I care so much that my ideas about life are understood by others?

Be willing to try to understand the moment instead of needing to be understood in it. You will lose yourself, and you will begin to have the great bliss of disappearing from your own life. At first, as you are willing to work to understand others more than you want to be understood by them, it seems a diminishing experience. But you will grow through this kind of self-negation into a new sense of yourself that actually includes all of life. You will begin to have a completely different relationship with everyone around you because you are no longer bringing yourself first and foremost into every relationship.

Helping Ourselves and Others
Break the Circle of Suffering

There is one incorruptible law, a cornerstone truth in the foundation of all relationships, that must be realized by each of us as being true for each of us if we wish to help ourselves and others grow in what is good for all. And since this law represents principle, there is no escaping its perfect justice. The wise person comes to love this law because through it he is granted freedom from wanting to hurt those who trespass against him, as well as from unknowingly hurting himself through his embrace of negative reactions. What is this perfect, incorruptible, self-liberating law? *Whatsoever we give to others, we first give to ourselves.*

Perhaps this truth has a familiar ring to you? It should. Who hasn't heard the timeless ideas that urge us to "Love thy neighbor as thyself," or "Do unto others as you would have them do unto you"? These words, and others in their vein, represent this one particular great truth that continually surfaces on this earth like the flowers of an eternal spring. It is not a mere positive aphorism meant to blossom and pass away. This law (and others like it) is the actual celestial stuff of those spiritual "wings" that make it possible for us to rise above our own nature as well as to help others realize this miracle. But before we can realize this power for the higher good it is, and that it grants, we must individually come into the truth of it. And to enter the truth (of anything) requires direct interaction, deep involvement, with what we would know in this way.

For instance, haven't we all held a wish at one time or another that the person who hurt us—as he did with that cruel remark or angry action—could know what we felt in that moment of their thoughtlessness? Somehow we just know that if this person could be present in our aching heart he would be more than just "sorry" *because he would share our sorrow*; and that out of this new order of relationship he could never and *would* never act so carelessly again.

Yet, for all of this higher self-understanding we think others should possess, we often fail to see our own spiritual poverty—how when we hurt someone with our own callous behavior we are unable to remember how much it hurt us to be on the receiving end of such scalding remarks. Where is this compassionate understanding when we really need it? How do we forget so quickly to be the kind of person we blame others for *not* being when they turn on us? To reveal the true nature of this sudden form of spiritual amnesia requires some soul searching of a kind. We must try to see, through our mind's eye, the workings of our own psychology in these moments where someone hurts us. To begin with, let's collect a few honest facts about what is taking place on our side of the duel that characterizes any unpleasant encounter with someone else.

First we need to acknowledge that when someone acts thoughtlessly toward us, it is a similar thoughtlessness in us that responds. In other words, our own hostile reactions take no thought for anything outside of what they call into account for their suddenly heated existence—so that the only awareness we possess in these times is that low level of cognizance that possesses us, making us "entitled" to attack back! And with our own aching heart or pounding thoughts providing the fuel, we lash out. After all, it is our "right" to set the record straight.

But in these moments, if we could learn to step back from ourselves—to see and to be aware of ourselves as being but a cog in this ever-turning wheel of hurting and being hurt— there would follow a great and liberating self-revelation. We would see, clearly, that before we rise up and attempt to hurt someone who has hurt us, it is we who hold this hurt first. And if we realize the dynamic exposed here—how one hurt always gives rise to another one—then we should also be able to see that each of us is always the first to hold this unwanted pain.

If we see the truth of this unconscious cycle, then we are ready for the next truth we will need to escape this circle of suffering: It doesn't matter how, or where, this dark cycle got started. It is not important any longer. Why? Because once we understand that to try to hurt someone—even just to want to—is to hurt ourselves, it makes no difference who did what to whom, or for whatever reasons. Once we come aware to the fact that when we hate, we feel this hatred first in ourselves, our relationship with this darkness is done. The whole issue becomes as simple as this: Hatred hurts us, not the person we blame for it. To hold a wish to punish someone begins with the unconscious embrace of the very pain we wish to inflict.

These discoveries all tell one story: Nothing grows on a battlefield except for the number of cries. Nothing can develop in us as long as the truth about our condition remains buried beneath so much misunderstanding. The point is that the pain we pass onto one another must stop somewhere or this cycle of conflict will never cease. And it must, or else the vital energies we need to grow beyond ourselves will simply be poured back into the earth for purposes unknown to us, even as we are compelled to serve conflict's dark plan through our unconscious suffering. What is the alternative?

Most of us already suspect what needs to be done if we are to have any hope of moving beyond the conflict so common in today's relationships. Nevertheless, here is a brief description of the spiritual action to be taken: We must stop giving to our friends and family the pain we cannot bear to carry ourselves. Said differently, each of us must agree to be the one who will "taste" what we would serve to our "enemy du jour" before we throw it upon his or her plate. Here is an example of how we can begin this new kind of inner work based in a higher kind of understanding about ourselves.

Whenever someone says something cruel, or otherwise does the unthinkable to us, our position toward this hurtful event is "calculated" right within our ensuing reaction to it—a reaction that describes to us the nature of the perceived attack even as it formulates a response to it. But no negative reaction of ours can read this moment any more than a tractor can pick up a copy of *Farm News* and study the feed prices reported in it. Our red-seeing reactions read only the content of their own right to exist. Their report, all based upon turbulent thoughts and feelings, tells us there is no choice but to return this pain right away or perish ourselves. These lower states cannot possibly see that this person they urge us to pounce on *is already in the hands of some pain* or he or she would never have thrown this suffering our way. And, perhaps most important of all, this same reactionary self will never understand this one inescapable fact of its own fury: With every pain it hurls back at its adversary, all it does is condemn itself to continue cycling through the level of ignorance that produces this pain to begin with. So, with each blow this unconscious nature delivers, it just creates for itself the need for the next set of blows.

Let it stop *now*. From this moment forward, let it stop with *you*. Make it your intention to forever quit yourself from the turning of this invisible wheel-of-woe. Each time we will consciously refuse to strike back in anger or act out some aggression toward the one who hurts us, we sow the seed of a new order of a conscious life. Now instead of being used by dark forces that grow at the expense of our soul's development, it is we who use our endless differences with others to grow endlessly. And at the same time that we learn to rise above the pain of our own negative reactions, we create the possibility and opportunity for others around us to do the same.

Each time we will choose not to respond to someone's mental or emotional blow with a blow of our own, that person is left no choice but to see that the only antagonist he has is his own pain. And just as this person's awakening to the continual cause of his unconscious aching is the beginning of the end of it, so too is this true for us. Our newly awakened understanding reveals that there is nothing for us to do with our pain but to let it be nothing to us. And with each such spiritual step that we will dare to take outside the circle of suffering, so do we make a way for everyone else . . . because at last the circle has been broken.

eleven

Life's Secret Lessons About Real Success

Counter to popular opinion, real success is *not* measured by the amount of our possessions. Simply stated, the truth is that real success— ultimately the *only* success—is determined by how much we are in actual possession of ourselves. And by the light of this great fact of life, we can also see that the person who fears the loss of what he thinks is his success has not truly succeeded. Why is this the truth? The individual who lives with secret self-defining fears is not a self-possessing person but rather a person possessed, often pushed and punished by his fears.

To see the truth of these findings is to realize the need for a whole new way to succeed in life. And to come upon this new order of success calls to us to search out a totally different path through life, a new path we can climb only by calling on a whole new set of higher actions. We can begin our ascent to securing real success with the following new action:

We must begin the inner work of consciously proving to ourselves that there is nothing to fear, instead of allowing our fears to push us into a never-ending series of fearful actions. This suggested new action makes more sense the more we gain insight into our present notion of success; for if we look closely, we can see that contained right within it, although unseen at present, is the fear of failure. The real fear behind this idea of failing is our unconscious fear of losing our familiar, confident sense of self. So, what we must see here, unflinchingly, is this next fact in our study.

As long as what we think of as being our "success" in life harbors the secret fear of our self somehow being diminished by the loss of this same external source, then our sense of self does not belong to us. Under these conditions we are little more than unsuspecting victims subject to every vagrant wind of change that blows through the world of our enterprise . . . not a very pleasant or promising prospect, is it? Of course not. But it doesn't have to be this way. We can learn life's secret lessons about the nature of real success, and follow them all the way to the Real Life that is their source. So let us begin this inner journey that will take us beyond our fears and our unconsciously fearing self.

There is a rather famous old World War II song entitled "Off We Go Into the Wild Blue Yonder." One of the reasons this song became memorable is that its lyrics touched on something deep in the human heart.

The only lyric I can remember from this song is sufficient to make my point: "Off we go/into the wild blue yonder/

flying high into the sky." Coupled with its emotionally rising melody, the idea seeded into these words speaks to our inherent longing to be free of limitations, to reach into uncluttered, open spaces within ourselves wherein all is free and filled with promise.

Everyone senses we are intended to be free creatures, to be able to roam and enjoy ever-widening spaces without the fear of falling. And even if we are not conscious of this sentiment, or perhaps even scoff at its idea, nevertheless we still experience our pleasures and pains as an effect of this unfettered consciousness within us.

Think about this for a moment. How else do we explain why we so often feel as though we are not free? Or that we are somehow unwilling captives of our own life? How can we know what something is not, or sense what we are not, unless there stands within us, at the same time, that which is this very state of self we feel is missing?

Freedom, real freedom, does exist. But it is not a condition of events, nor is it found within another person's approval of us. Neither is real freedom ever a mere effect of circumstances, otherwise it is not freedom but merely a temporary pleasure we have mistaken for being the same as being free.

What, then, is real freedom? Where is it to be found? Let us start by saying that freedom is a quality of Truth, one of its great branches. And as it has been so timelessly spoken of, it is in realizing the truth of ourselves that we are set free. This is why there is no substitute for the true self-knowledge that follows.

Our present self often feels itself captive because the only way it can "know" itself is through the unconscious comparison of its past experiences to its present circumstances. In other words, this level of self only knows what it is once it has gazed into the mirror of what it was. This realm of reflections represents its entire range of existence.

Anytime life brings along an event that can't be neatly fit into the pre-set realm of this self, it immediately gets shaky. Suddenly finding itself unable to be certain as to the meaning of the unwanted moment, this lower level of self fears the loss of its imagined control. The way it deals with this fear— in order to regain its lost "powers"—is to mentally reconfigure its reality until once again comfortable in its self-constructed kooky kingdom. But here is the point of describing all of this to you.

Without our awareness of this interior kingdom and its covert operations that keep us captive, we are little more than prisoners confined to the limitations of this level of consciousness. But this construed consciousness is not our True Consciousness. Stated another way, this limited realm at the root of our present reality is not the whole Kingdom available to us. It is in our seeing the truth of this, and what it intimates to us about the potential of our True Self, that the path to freedom is revealed. For now we know: We must leave this self behind. And this action requires learning to take conscious, spiritual risks. What is a spiritual risk?

A spiritual risk is any action we will take based upon our willingness to challenge our own certainty that our present state of consciousness represents the full measure of life's possibility. Here is one simple example for our study: Maybe we feel as though no one understands our situation or that no one is being sensitive to the pressure we're under. During these times most of us feel the strong need to complain to someone—anyone (including ourselves)—in order to win some sympathy. The conscious risk in this case is to give no voice to any complaints, either outwardly or inwardly.

Whenever we feel ourselves certain that we are a captive of something—be it anything from a fear of proceeding with a wish we have, to that feeling of being inadequate to getting through a task at hand—we remember in this same self-defining moment that this reality before our eyes is, at best, only a partial one. And then, as unthinkable as it seems to us in this same moment, as certain as we may feel that real freedom is beyond our reach, we make the conscious leap into the Wild New Yonder. What does this mean? What is the Wild New Yonder?

Once we realize that our present view of self, a view that defines our reality, is a construct of a certain level of our own consciousness—one that's convinced the limit of its present view is the limit of its possibility—we also realize the need to leave this self-limited world behind us.

Knowing the makeup of this world we must abandon, we have but one choice: Let go of who we are sure we are and make a leap into the Wild New Yonder. Our new and conscious choice is to discover what awaits us in the open-ended reality, instead of allowing ourselves to be grounded by a preconceived notion of who we are and what we can do.

Nothing can stop us from taking this leap into all that we may be, other than this mistaken and unconscious conviction we have of who we already are—a mindset supported by the strange comfort we find in clinging to who we have been.

Find the places in your life where you can take these conscious, spiritual risks. The liberation you win will be the repeated discovery that the only thing holding you captive is yourself. Make nothing more valuable than your inner work to enter into the Wild New Yonder.

Living Free Above Success and Failure

When I read the Bible, I have comfort followed by guilt in some passages, i.e., "It's easier for a camel to pass through the eye of a needle than a rich man to enter the kingdom of heaven." I am torn about what "making it" really means. Is it wrong to want to be successful?

What each of us must do, if we are ever to be truly successful human beings, is learn to ask what the results are that we are seeking. Being spiritually asleep as we are, when a certain thought passes through our mind, along with a certain emotional content and image, we believe that the picture we have there in our mind is what we really want. But the truth is that we have all had one reward after another in obtaining what we imagined, yet we are still hungry for more. If this much begins to get clear—that we live from a nature that is a bottomless basket (and we see the results of this nature in the world around us)—then we begin to question the "results" it seeks. We see that these results are not only unattainable but untenable as well. As we drop the drives that belong to our highly conditioned nature, we gradually discover that the result we wanted all along was there all along—to be our own person, and to have our own life, free of the insanity of ambitious competition and all the rest.

Then we have succeeded. And best of all, the Truth that makes this possible then sees to it that we have the rest of what we need.

Are failures in life inevitable? Does the higher power, once attained, see to it that we only succeed?

Try to understand the difference between living from something within yourself, whose nature is contentment itself, and living from those parts of yourself that are forever seeking contentment. For the man or woman who persists with the wish for Truth/God to be first in life, there really is no such thing as failure. Why? Because every action taken under the auspices of this inner wish purifies the person holding it in his or her heart—leaving greater clarity and more inward certainty about what forwards the Truth's action and what hinders it. In short, the person begins to win true Wisdom, with its infallible Intelligence.

Is there ever a time when we should set goals and plan for our future, or does our developing awareness reveal what is needed on a moment-to-moment basis?

We must all learn what it means to understand scale and levels. At certain points in our life, it may be that goals and plans are necessary. Perhaps we have children, and so we need to provide for family, or we want a special education, and so we must decide upon a series of steps to take. But for most of us, our goals and plans revolve around ambitions to be someone special, to own special things. These goals and plans, even when realized, simply leave us having to devise another set of goals and plans. Then, maybe one day, we see that these kinds of goals and plans are secret punishments.

In that moment we outgrow the self that thought it knew what was needed. Now we can begin to listen for new instructions from a higher part of ourselves.

The idea that we should "take no thought for the morrow" sounds great . . . to live each moment as it is . . . yet how can we practice this and still set goals for ourselves?

It is not a question of setting goals and having directives versus being spiritually awake. The real issue is the right order of things. Being awake and self-aware must come before personal goals; otherwise, the nature setting those goals may have an agenda contrary to Real Life. One level of self feels it cannot be fulfilled without continually reinventing a new future for itself wherein it is at last a "winner," while our True Nature rests content in reality and *knows* now that it *already* possesses everything it needs. We must choose which of these natures we will nourish.

My spiritual studies lead me to believe that goal setting is an exercise in futility, but the success training I receive at work indicates that goal setting is vital for personal growth. Are the two philosophical systems opposed, or am I confused?

The two systems run into conflict (as they almost must) when we set goals that we unconsciously set our sense of self-worth within. Then these goals become punishments even if we achieve them, because as they change—as life changes—we feel a sense of loss. Setting practical goals is not antithetical to spiritual success; trying to be someone special is.

How possible is it to excel at something (i.e., art, music, philosophy, or even politics) without being driven by unconscious forces?

Your question points to something very deep. When we are "driven," it is always to arrive at some point wherein we will no longer feel as though something is missing in us. All such drives in us are doomed at the outset. Here's why: These compulsive states of self are the unconscious expression of the opposites within us where the insufficient self we think ourselves to be projects a time and place where we won't be this same self anymore. This divided state of self produces conflict, frustration, and ultimately disappointment, because no opposite can resolve itself. On the other hand, when it is the love of something that motivates us and moves us, that love—for whatever the endeavor may be—is its own reward in the moment. This is the real definition of success. Here there is no future and no past to escape. And best of all, Love is the perfect self-purifier, which means each action taken under its direction elevates the one so directed.

Right Livelihood Along the Path to Self-Liberation

How does one know that they are in their true vocation in life? My interests wander so much at times, but I know one thing for sure: I don't feel the true satisfaction and peace that I think I should feel in life.

Let me answer you differently than you might expect. The quality of our life is first and foremost an expression of the level of our understanding. Without self-understanding, you could be the king of this planet and you would still feel empty and unfulfilled. With self-understanding, whatever you do has a life within it. This life born of higher self-understanding is fulfillment itself. "Seek ye first" means all things good come to those for whom the good is all things.

> I am taking the biggest risk of my life and am about to leave a long-standing job for a new home-business opportunity. Although I have basically kept my old job out of fear, there is quite a bit of fear in leaving the safety of the known for the unknown. Any ideas on how to make this new adjustment in life and how to quell the uncertainty?

Here is a good tip in general when it comes to getting ready to step into anything unknown: Strive to do what is in your power while remaining awake to what is not. It is not in your power to control what will occur or how events will transpire. But it is in your power to be awake to the fearful voices that either project some doom or that denounce you for making mistakes. Realize that these fearful states are secretly trying to keep you captive. The only hold they have is the fear they can get you to buy into about "you." Remember: Do what is in your power, not what is not.

> I feel bored with my job and my life in general. In the past I would have looked for a new job or a time-consuming hobby. Is the boredom a "false self" feeling or is it a legitimate feeling? Can self-understanding clear up the boredom, or should I take outward steps to do so?

Boredom is the "natural" effect of the thought nature having begun to exhaust its own content. What this means to us is that when we are bored with life, it is because we have at last begun to outgrow what our thought-life can provide for us. Your suspicion about not trying to answer it is correct. Stay in the middle of this condition. It may be appropriate or not to make changes, but wait until it is quite clear to you that what you newly intend is not part of the old line of your life.

> **I am a recent college graduate and ironically, although I went to school for one thing, I am no longer sure I want to do it. How can I find something I really love to do and know it is the right course?**

Do not put the cart before the horse. Be patient. Try to remain as open as possible to the different impressions you receive when considering a livelihood. The odds are you do know what you love, but this right intuition is getting all confused in the presence of the other socially driven voices in you that call out to you to fulfill their agenda. These parts of a person would have him believe that to be happy, he must win the approval of the world for the work he does. This is where everything gets turned around in our lives. It is impossible to find real happiness and abiding contentment in this life without love. If something you love calls to you, you may be assured that it has prepared for you everything you need to be a confident, content, and spiritually whole human being. The physical aspects will take care of themselves.

> **Regarding knowing one's vocation, some people seem to really have a passion for what they do, but I don't think that necessarily means they know themselves any better than the rest of us.**

Yes. Some people do have passion for what they do, and it often does not necessarily mean that they know themselves any better than the rest of us. We must all be willing to subject our passions to the internal scrutiny of our (hopefully) awakening consciences. Many people are passionate for what they do because they are in the grip of unconscious fears telling them that unless they run here or do this, they are going to lose something of value. When we really love something, *really* love it, that love itself is the value and the reward. This is why, incidentally, the love of God is the perfect love.

Pull Yourself Out of the World's Pull on You

How can one possibly deal with the outer world's daily duties, and still strive to go deep into the inner world to find peace?

Diving into the outer world, with all of its daily obligations, and striving to go deeply into one's self are not contradictory ideas. Our present mind sees it this way, but when we will work with true principles, it is right in the midst of the storms that we discover shelter. This shelter has always been there, only waiting to be entered as we see that all storms are self-creations.

My one wish is to become fully awake. It is my work and passion to understand my true nature and to manifest that fully and uncompromisingly. I have experienced such wondrous moments in my journey. On the other hand, much to my dismay, I have to work at a job that demands efforts to succeed. When involved this way my mind can't stay in the present moment. What do I need to know at this juncture?

As our inner work flourishes, there grows a natural vacillation between practical thought and awareness of self. Where we presently live within ourselves is in an unconscious oscillation between scattered thoughts and negative emotions. As you work to remain aware of yourself, you will find that the awakened state will visit you more regularly. As this happens, you will find that you can stay more easily self-aware and awake (even while at work, and even in the midst of practical thought) because this new and higher energy grants you this ability. In short, there is no essential conflict between our wish to stay awake and the work we must do in the world. If anything, the more awake we can be, the more successful we will be in all areas of work.

> My concerns for running a sound business and making a decent living for my family seem to prevent me from pursuing a spiritual life. The fear of not having enough drives my life. I am confused about what my true purpose should be, and I long to strike a balance between worldly concerns and spiritual growth.

The issues you raise about how your business concerns seem to be in conflict with your wish for a progressive inner life are a source of confusion to many seekers. The only real confusion we face at any time is over what our purpose is here on this earth. Please don't think this an oversimplification of the problem. Whenever we are unsure about what this life is for, we invent images to supply this missing certainty. One of these images, and a more common one these days, may be to picture ourselves as "successful" businesspeople, or experts who are looked up to and held in high esteem by others. Living from this purpose, our sense of self is all wrapped up in making our enterprises succeed, for we believe our security—in fact, in some ways our very "life"—depends upon keeping the picture intact. So our time and energies, physically and psychologically, are absorbed by this image and its intended goal. Our business now runs us. Unfortunately, this goal to "win" is powerless to produce what it promises, and actually serves to divide us—a state that prohibits spiritual success. Now we find ourselves at odds with our own inventions. And while I realize this illustration may sound extreme to you, as your stated wish was to learn how to strike a balance between necessary worldly concerns and spiritual growth, nevertheless, the principle governing our inner success remains true here as well.

Imagine a man picking apples in his orchard, which happens to sit in the wilds somewhere. He must pick fruit to survive, and yet he knows that each time he ventures out into his orchards his life is in danger, for mountain lions roam the region. I ask you to tell me: Where would this man's attention be the whole time he was busy with his worldly duty? That's right. He would go to work each time with the understanding that his task in his world of trees is always a twofold one: the first to be awake for signs of danger, the second to enjoy the fruits his efforts may produce for him. In short, awareness of his true condition defines his purpose, and it is this purpose that sets, or tends to define, what his genuine priorities are.

Our efforts to do good, sound business do not have to be, as our false nature would have us believe, at the cost of being awake and enjoying the natural fruits of spiritual goodness. Let us each resolve, as many times as needed, to redefine what we really want from this life, and in the light of our renewed, higher purpose, place our attention to those areas of our inner life that this new purpose demands. When we live in this way, with Truth as our intention and truthfulness as our guide, there is no more conflict.

As far as what to do about those fears of not having enough to live the way you want to, ask yourself the following question: Can anything I am afraid to live without ever be the source of my fearlessness? The answer is obviously a resounding "No!" But what does this discovery teach us? What good is anything we may have if all it can do for us is make us frightened that one day we may not have enough of "it" . . . whatever that "it" may be—money, approval, family, friends, etc.? We must get tired of being frightened that one day we may not have enough of what it is in our lives that has failed and is powerless to make us fearless human beings. Then, as it grows clear to us that our problem is fear itself, we will know exactly what to do each time we start to feel afraid. We will become consciously fearless. We will be aware of the fear, but no longer buy into what it wants us to do about it. Here begins the truly fearless life.

Mother Theresa once said, "The more you have, the less you have to give." Would it be good for us to be poor? Why do physical possessions seem to have this "corruptive" nature that is so antithetical to the spiritual life?

In a word: identification. Now add to this idea what it means to be attached to things. We are never attached to the objects themselves; rather, we are attached to the sense of self we derive from our ideas about these objects as to what they "make us." Goodness has nothing to do with either poverty or wealth relative to this world and its possible possessions. There is a poverty that true spiritual aspirants discover, but it has nothing to do with ownership or the lack of it. This poverty is the discovery that we had mistaken ourselves to be something we were not. This realization is the beginning of real riches.

> **I have heard it said that we are spiritual beings having a human experience, but if we were spiritual beings having a human experience, wouldn't we know it?**

Think about what you have asked for a moment. We do know it. We realize it almost every day through our dissatisfaction with our human experience. All of us long for what is eternal. The human experience is an exercise in letting go . . . saying goodbye to everything temporary that we mistook for being timeless.

Three Steps to Success Without Stress

Here is a short exercise that is designed to help you take the spiritual risks necessary to win your freedom and realize real success. It will be your responsibility to find the "right" moments to take each inner leap, but your willingness to work with these steps to higher self-success will prove invaluable.

Whenever confronted with something before you that produces within you feelings of limitation, however they are expressed (such as some fear or sense of futility), remember the three simple instructions below. Follow them as best you can, but be sure to stay awake to those mechanical impulses that want you to just go through the motions instead of being an active participant in the workings of your own inner life.

First Step: Look Up

What does this mean? Look beyond yourself to your new and higher understanding that there already exists a Wild New Yonder right within you. You can help yourself succeed at this by remembering there is always something higher than whatever your present self calls its reality. If it helps, remember God, or His light, or that Truth always prevails. The key here is to recall that there does exist an open-ended world of new possibilities even as all you are experiencing and perceiving is the shrinking cell of your self.

Second Step: Let Go

Just drop your certainty that you can't make it into the Wild New Yonder by realizing that the parts active in you in this moment, the temporary person in charge of your life, has no interest in breaking free of itself. What once was (the past) has absolutely no power to affect what is (the Now) once you choose to stand upon this self-renewing ground of self-newness. Let go of what you are sure you can't do, and make the leap into being willing to find out the truth of yourself. Besides, it should be evident by now. Unless we first quit what has been defeating us, how can we arrive at the new order of success that we long for?

Third Step: Leap!

Just jump. Take the action you are sure you can't. Step out of yourself and into the Wild New Yonder. When we realize that all we really risk when daring to challenge whatever confines us is little more than a mistaken concept of ourselves, what is there to hold us down? Nothing! And this understanding is the seed of our new success.

Just beyond who you are sure you are is another whole order of self that has none of the restrictions of which your present self feels itself a captive. But you must agree to the journey that begins with this jump! Real success is the discovery that real freedom exists within you. Practice makes perfect, so go to work. Practice these principles of success until their hidden purpose reveals their hidden powers.

twelve

Principles and Practices Along the Path to Self-Awakening

There is one principle and telling practice that has woven its way through the bedrock of every true religion since the beginning of time. This supreme principle and practice is to the true religious life it reflects what the ocean is to the rivers that flow into it and then return again through the perfect course of nature's cycle.

What we may call this principle and practice has as many names as does that Supreme Intelligence whose purpose it serves, and yet it remains as unnameable as the One with no name whom we endeavor to touch and be touched by through our inner work.

The short story you are about to read reveals the heart of this principle and practice.

If you will read it with a wish to learn its truth, you can't help but catch a glimpse of the secret nature of this same self-perfecting principle and practice.

There was once a prosperous country ruled by a wise king. His singular desire was that the great wealth of his kingdom be shared with any of its citizens who were found rightfully worthy. And so, to grant his own compassionate wish, the good king established an annual Festival of Fidelity—a solid week of fun and feasting, concluding with a special three-day-long contest.

During the contest time, each citizen was given a chance to take the courtyard's center stage, and there to profess to the assembled masses and various ministers his or her love for the kingdom. Then, after all who so desired to speak were given their chance, in a selection process known only to the king himself, a winner was announced. The following evening, in a glorious ceremony, the highly coveted prize of prizes was awarded: permanent title in the royal court, which included all of the benefits attending such a noble position. As you might imagine, competition was intense.

One day, on the eve of the great Festival of Fidelity, the king's youngest daughter came to him and politely requested permission to ask a special question of him.

"What is it, my princess?" the king responded.

"Father," she said somewhat pensively, "as you've asked, I've attended many of the Festival contests like the one starting tomorrow. And each year I find myself moved by so many of the speakers that choosing the best would be impossible for me. I know you to be wise and fair in all things, as all of the previous winners have thus proven themselves loyal and true to you and the kingdom. And yet I have no idea how you reach the decision you do."

Then she lifted her eyes up to his, which she realized had been intently watching hers all along. After a short hesitation, she finished her thought:

"Won't you please tell me how you choose the winner?"

The king continued looking into her eyes and then, reaching his decision, spoke the following words:

"Those who come to the contest late, and who leave early, make their appearance and their moving speeches not for their love of kingdom, but rather for the selfish sake of having others see, or think of them, as being the one who loves king and country the most. Theirs is but an unseen, secret self-love, and as such, so runs their loyalty—in spite of all the moving words they use to tell a different story."

Knowing her father was teaching her more than she had asked for, yet grateful for the royal lesson, the princess figured the best approach was simply to continue her original line of questioning.

"If this is true of the many, then how *do* you choose the one most worthy citizen? Please, tell me your secret."

The king smiled to himself and, after looking around to ensure they were alone, began to speak quietly. "The morning of each day of the contest, being sure not to stir anyone else, I arise very early and disguise myself beyond recognition."

He could see his daughter's bright eyes start dancing about with obvious pleasure in learning of her father's secret fun. So he smiled back, openly, as if to admit his secret sport, and continued with his story. "I disguise myself in order to mingle amongst the throngs unnoticed, so that I can look for who will be the contest winner."

"Wait a minute," the princess spoke out, interrupting her father. "Are you saying that you select the winner *before* you've heard the contestants?"

He continued speaking, not so much ignoring her, but knowing that his original answer was still the answer she needed to hear in order to understand.

"On each of these three days, I wait and watch for that one-in-a-thousand citizen who alone arrives early and who lingers late for *all three days*; that man or women who, not unlike myself, is there in the courtyard with only one purpose in mind—whose *real reason* for being there is incidental to taking part in the speakers' contest."

His daughter moved forward on the cushioned chair where she sat, opening her eyes as wide as possible so as to ask, without having to ask, *What is this real reason?* What intention could be so special that it sets someone apart from the rest of the crowd, making him or her worthy of a court title? And the king answered:

"This rare citizen, who waits and watches daily in the courtyard, hopes for one thing, and one thing only: to catch a glimpse of their king, and then, maybe, to be near him for a moment, should Providence allow. This is the citizen I select, for their consistent actions show what they really love." He paused. And then he spoke slowly—deliberately, softly, but firmly.

"Learn, my little princess, before all else, to see what is true, and then little of what you hear will ever be able to mislead or painfully deceive you."

And then, in a way known only to fathers, the king reached out and took his daughter's hand in his own and asked, "Do you understand?"

"Yes, father. I believe that I do."

To summarize the principle revealed in this short story, the power of any spiritual practice is not derived from *what* we do—or by being seen doing it—but in *why* we do it. It is our *intention* alone that determines the course of our spiritual destiny and our success in realizing our higher aim.

Teachers, Teachings, and Tools Along the Spiritual Path

What role does organized religion play in "truth"?

As opposed to doing the required inner work to discover what is false about their present life, most people are very comfortable with organized religion because it allows them the ease of simply accepting what others say is true about the Almighty. Allowing any person or organization to act as a middleman between you and your God is spiritual death. To accept any truth as being so—that you have not personally awakened to and found to be true in your own life—is the path to a wrongful self-righteousness and all forms of harmful hypocrisy. The purpose of Moses, Christ, Buddha, Mohammed, and all truly illuminated beings is to give individuals their heavenly rights to be free, not to create groups of slaves calling themselves free.

I have been noticing more and more "enlightened" people. My experience with esoteric studies makes me skeptical of too much enlightenment, but I sense that I don't yet know how to tell true from false. What is to prevent me from latching onto some false teaching that masquerades as truth?

This is an increasingly important issue in these days where everyone has a card that introduces him or her as some master or avatar. We can only recognize what is false in others to the degree that we have uncovered that same nature within ourselves. As we work and root out what is untrue, it becomes easier and easier to instantly taste the truth of anything (or anyone) we encounter. Do your own work. Go inward. Be alone. Ask the Supreme for help and guidance, as best you understand how to ask and from what spirit to ask this. If you will do your work this way, a part of you will develop that could no more be fooled by a false light than a moth would fly into a dark well.

Does the physical proximity of a teacher of truth to the student have a lot of importance?

There is no doubt that proximity to a teacher of Truth accelerates one's inner development. However, and equally important to understand, a true teacher simply represents in this physical life what already exists within the seeker in his or her invisible spiritual life. Our work is to make contact with Truth/Christ/God. And right where you are is where this nature dwells at this moment. Wake up. Ask for something higher and then be receptive to the ensuing response of life. It never fails to come.

How do we discern whether or not we are associated with a qualified spiritual guide on the path to God?

There is an old saying that goes, "It takes a lighted candle to light a candle." This is deeply true and important for seekers to understand. Unfortunately, true guides are as rare as hen's teeth, but this doesn't mean that an individual's wish to awaken into relationship with the Supreme must be halted. Equally important, in fact a necessity in being able to discern true teachings from the abundant false ones, is one's true wish to become a new man or woman. The Truth is the great purifier. And those who will continue to put the Truth first will not only reach their wish for a higher life, but that Truth will go before them to reveal the difference between what is light and what is dark.

What specific techniques or practices help to foster internal development and reduce the effects of our ego nature?

Our present nature is very fragmented, with many parts all clamoring to take charge and direct us, so learning to quiet the mind and to properly discipline the body are important steps in reducing these overall negative effects upon us. Before we can hope to realize higher influences, we must first become conscious of, and separate ourselves from, these conflicted aspects of ourselves. Meditation, yoga, a prayer life, nature walks, being balanced physically . . . all of these things help a person's development. Physical and spiritual practices can be a valuable aid to us, as long as we don't mistake the means for the end.

Are spiritual study groups useful, or should we venture forward on our own?

We must venture forward on our own, but much can be gained by working with like-minded, serious spiritual aspirants. So the answer to your question is not whether or not a group is valuable, but whether or not there is value in the group.

Why is it so difficult for those who have awakened to tell those of us not more realized what their world is like?

The candle in the night thought herself illuminated until she was placed next to the flames of the fireplace. The fire in her place was sure no one could be brighter until the full moon rose in the window, and the moon believed she was the light itself until she witnessed the morning sunrise.

Spiritual Practices and the Presence of God

Is having a silent mind essential to spiritual development, and what exactly is gained by practicing inner silence?

True silence is not just the absence of noise; it is a kind of spiritual medium in which not only are we able to discern what is false, but through which what is true can increasingly reach us and teach us. It is very helpful to practice some form of being silent. As you develop a "taste" for inner quiet, you will not only long more for this silent friend, but you will find new ways to bring it along with you wherever you go. The fundamental purpose of spending time in quiet or silence is to make clear to ourselves all of the many relationships that we are continually experiencing in thoughts and feelings within ourselves without knowing it. As we work at being quiet and stepping back from ourselves, we begin to realize that there is an "I" or sense of self that exists apart from all of this inner company. Eventually, we will find ourselves effortlessly centered within this silent self. When this occurs, and as this occurs, we enjoy the sense of strength and comfort that comes with knowing ourselves apart from any of the temporary inner visitors we formerly took ourselves to be. Keep practicing.

What is meditation, and is there some "best" method for its practice?

Real meditation is our willingness and work to be aware of what we are in relationship with within ourselves twenty-four hours a day. To answer what is the best method of meditation, we must first understand the purpose of meditation. True meditation allows us to enter into relationship and to be with those parts of ourselves that await us within and above ourselves. This new order of self-unity—where the observer perceives his oneness with the observed—is realized through *conscious awareness*, the true foundation of *all* forms of meditation. With this in mind, the notion of a "best" form of meditation becomes simple and personal: Find the practice that best fulfills the continuous flowering of this awareness.

I have been working on "prayer without ceasing," but at times feel as though I am just being a parrot. How does the practice of ceaseless prayer relate to Christ's admonition to avoid vain repetitions? It seems at times that I am dividing my attention by this practice.

Don't be a parrot. That is what Christ meant by not doing vain repetitions. He was simply instructing people not to move from one mechanical life into another. The practice of ceaseless prayer is a means to an end, not a way of defining ourselves. Lastly, if you are awake, attentive to your inner and outer life (which is the purpose of this practice), it unifies rather than divides attention.

> **My biggest fear at the moment is that I am incapable of ever experiencing true spirituality. My mind will never be quiet. I have no patience, and I'm attracted to everything that glitters! And yet, in spite of these conditions that hold me captive, I wish for a more spiritual life. Where do I begin?**

The upper path begins in the moment where the lower path is no longer tolerable. In other words, we begin this inner work whenever we recognize the futility of our past actions. But to this thought we must add one other: We can't begin to recognize a futile action as being such without seeing the self responsible for selling us that action. As we see ourselves as we are, the natural longing for the wisdom we need to act differently, to be different, is spontaneously awakened in us. This is our guide. It is unfailing. Don't be concerned with how you will or won't succeed. Pay attention instead to where you let yourself invest yourself in what is inherently a dead end.

> **Should we only pray for the help we need to realize our God, or can prayer be used to request other things, such as healings for friends or better life circumstances?**

Prayer is a vehicle. Think of it that way. There is no doubt that our prayers can help others, but only as long as that prayer has its basis in something genuine. On the other hand, praying for better "things" in your life arises from an unconscious nature within you, a divided nature that thinks it can escape its constricted or limited world by holding onto one end of the rope and trying to climb the other. Every problem or sense of limitation that we have has an answer. And that answer lies within discovering our true nature. If we will "seek the Kingdom," then all else truly does follow. Within each individual waits an incomprehensibly large world. It is in the discovery of this greater Kingdom within us that the problems we face appear as they really are, which is to say we discover that they are small or of no real consideration.

> I know this will sound a bit strange but I feel I'd be happier if I could only find a way to spend more quality time by myself, with myself. Yet I fear silence. How can I develop a deeper relationship with silence?

How did you fall in love with anyone the first time? Something about that person captivated you. Something in that person had something—a quality—that nourished you. Falling in love with silence happens naturally as you spend more time cultivating your relationship with her. Within silence is a whole new world, new qualities, and a new order of love. Seek her.

The Christian Path to Higher Consciousness

> I have seen so much hypocrisy and violence done in the name of God that I have never felt attracted to any organized system of religious belief. I have concerns that one can become too dependent on the idea of God and Christ.

There is no real need on anyone's part to "believe" in anything. Reality (or God) is not dependent upon belief. What is necessary on our part is to pursue the Truth. Christ's life, the real meaning of it (and not the nightmare it has become distorted to be), has nothing to do with belief, but with relationship. His teachings, and that of all other true teachers, have always stressed that we see life as it really is and therein find what awaits us. The nicest thing about being a truth seeker is that each step of the way that we will take with the sincere wish to learn the truth about this life reveals that same truth. As far as becoming dependent upon God, that is like saying you don't want to depend on air to breathe! The concept of God is where the danger of dependency lies. When we see through all concepts for what they are, as it concerns our spiritual work, then we also see through self—that false self that is the secret opposite of the concepts it clings to for spiritual safety.

> **Christ, however he is construed, was not alone in the Great Work of helping humans to awaken. Buddha, Moses, Mohammed . . . all of these prophets brought forth evidence of a higher purpose in life, a plan at work in our lives to realize this truth of ourselves. Don't these traditions have a place in our spiritual work?**

The great traditions can be a source of encouragement and knowledge as we awaken to ourselves. But tradition, regardless of its depth and breadth, is only (and should be only) a part of our work. Our task is to connect with the same Celestial Consciousness that stirred the great men and women who blazed the trails that are now tradition. We must walk the trail, not the tradition. Christ was first a reformer of the spiritual life of man, then a reformer of the laws codifying this possibility. He used his own being to prove that we are, and do become, what we most love.

When I spoke to a close Christian friend of mine of the freedom I have begun to realize as a result of my new self-studies, he spoke his concerns for my eternal salvation. The issue is about the doctrine of the resurrection, and more specifically, Jesus' words: "I am the way, the truth, and the life; no man comes to the Father but by me." How are these things reconciled, and is there a way to discuss this subject with my friend?

The true Christ, apart from his life in Jesus, is not a person, but the Celestial Power of undivided Love. This Love is freedom. And this order of freedom is a gift for anyone who wearies of being a captive of himself. Heaven is not a time to come, just as Christ is not a future self. The Kingdom is within; it is not a thought, it is not a creed, it is not a belief, nor even a faith. It belongs to the man or woman who wants a real life. Christ himself always told his disciples, "Watch." The translation of this original Aramaic word is: "Be awake!" Don't try to convince anyone of anything, and be wary of anyone who wants you to embrace what they do through terror tactics. The odds are that if you look closely at this person warning you of hell, you would see that, in his fear, he is in it. Follow your wish to be free, not people who say they know where it is even as they are imprisoned in the imitative life. This natural longing you have for the light will blossom and, as it does, you will have Christ's life the way it was always intended.

What did Christ mean when he said we must take up our cross and follow him?

For the seeker of Life, the conversion from our embittered self—with its hardened heart—into a new man or woman requires a conscious compliance; it takes submission of self involving a willingness to endure our present nature as it ceases to be one form, even before it is transformed into another, higher one. Going through this conscious conversion is the "crucifixion," for the sweetness of God's own life comes only after the curing of our own. It follows the passing of that life we are in into a Life we cannot know in our present state. Here is the tearing of the fibers of our very self—not a maturing, but a gradual replacement—becoming new in the light of God's birth in us even as we feel ourselves dying to all that we have ever been or hope to be. Thus knowing that our will cannot be transformed, but only surrendered, does nothing to make the task of going through our conversion less painful, and yet it does make this life of waiting—and ripening on the vine—endurable.

New Light on the Lessons in the Bible

Are the laws in the Bible really God's, or are they man's interpretations? It seems that man destroys whatever he gets his hands on, so why should the Bible be any exception?

Yes, it is true that this world is twisted and upside down. We mustn't cast stones, but rather work to realize why this has happened. Even a cursory glance over our involvement with our Earth shows we are in wrong relationship with life, and with the truth of it as such. Throughout time our spiritual life has played a constant second fiddle to our aspirations and ambitions in this world. However, when we turn around (which is the original meaning of the word "repent"), then the Truth begins to reveal itself directly to us. Any other truths, other than the ones that have come to life within us and for us, become our secret captors. Work to awaken. Ask God to help you see the truth in all things. Then when you read the Bible, or any other great religious text, you will know from yourself whether those words were inspired or from authority-seeking, self-deceived power mongers.

When Jesus told his disciples that they must lose themselves to find themselves, was this the process of finding true self? Is the Bible a good resource for living truth?

Yes, we come upon our True Nature by continually awakening to who and what we are not. This is a real work process that is unmistakable to the self-working individual. As what we can no longer be becomes clearer to us, there is a kind of internal dying to ourselves; in this conscious self-passing arises a whole new sense of our being born through and in relationship with Christ/God. The Bible can be a wonderful source of wisdom and encouragement, as long as we realize that its teachings are intended to lead us to our own discoveries of Real Life, and not to provide us with a false sense of self and imagined security.

When Jesus told Thomas, "Blessed are those who believe and have not seen," did he mean that hope that is seen is not real hope?

As we work and awaken, we discover that we are already part of an Eternal Nature within which everything is done and perfectly supplied for us. These are not just words. As this Nature strengthens its presence within us, we don't see what we hope for, but rather we become that New Nature. We realize a oneness with the Truth that already knows "all is well." So, in a way, we start with hope that such a life exists, and somewhere down the road, this hope is strengthened— even as the self that knew itself through that hope begins to disappear. There is such a thing as real hope, but we must be vigilant and not mistake it for a sense of well-being supplied through yet another false hope. False hope is that one day you will escape yourself using your own best ideas and ambitions for self-release. Real hope begins with understanding that who you really are is already in relationship with God, and that the issue is not about hoping Him into your life, but discovering where it is that wrong parts of you are obscuring His presence.

When Jesus went into the desert to do battle with Satan, I always thought he was doing battle with himself. Isn't "Satan" actually our own false self?

First it must be stated—contrary to popular interpretations of this story—that Christ did not "battle" Satan. In one sense he corrected this powerful principality, even as he dismissed it from his presence. The only power any darkness has over any of us is in the absence of light within us. This story from the New Testament gives us knowledge to base our actions on, for within each of us dwell all created forms. It is through the God-given gift of awareness, of the Living Light, that we can discover and dismiss the presence of these eternal forces as they are acting upon us, and thereby choose in favor of what we will. Christ, the Light, dwells within us, as does darkness. It is our choice as to the relationships we foster, and we are made wiser by the results of each such choice.

Each generation thinks that the Book of Revelation is written exclusively for their time, hence, whatever catastrophe occurs means the end time to them. What is the true meaning of Revelation?

In a very certain sense, it is always "end time," a fact most of us realize, in scale, too late, each time we crash into the end of one false hope or another. At our present level of development, we perceive our life through a nature that is both a creation of time and that can see events only in time. In reality, everything is already done and is at the same time occurring. The spirit of Christ is now, not back then. The choice is now or never. Revelation is now, not a time to come. Therefore, end time is now, never-endingly. This is why our soul's task is to be awake and to choose the light, right side of life. Then all else good just happens.

Release Yourself by Realizing a New Order Within Yourself

As we have been discovering throughout the course of our truth studies together, awakening to Real Life occurs in direct proportion to waking up from our own sleeping nature—a fact which brings us face to face with some of life's oldest and greatest spiritual mysteries.

The myth of the phoenix, the riddle of the sphinx, even the story of Christ's birth in a dimly lit stable of barnyard animals . . . all point to the existence of one nature dwelling in the midst of another; of two separate orders of being merged in one relationship—one lower, one higher—one asleep to itself, the other awake, above, and in charge of its lesser parts. This invisible state of self must be realized before its relationship can be reversed and the sleeper awakens to his or her indwelling Spirit. To this end, we must learn to use each moment possible to awaken to ourselves instead of surrendering ourselves to our usual circle of dreams in which we alternate in appearance as either hero or villain.

Yet it is often right here, at the outset of our resolve to awaken to ourselves, where we run into an old foe: the "how-to" stumbling block, an ancient barrier created by the very same level of mind we wish to awaken from. And this stage of our self-development brings us to another fascinating fact along the path to self-awakening: The path before us is paved with pitfalls for the unwary, where what others would have us believe is true—or otherwise tell us what we must do to awaken—becomes itself a barrier and a part of the very limitation within ourselves that we set out to transcend. So let it be known that far more important to our inner success than coming upon these so-called secret "how-to" practices, or those who would teach them, is our own awakening awareness of our need to come awake. For though we may be (and often are) deceived, this divine need in us cannot be deceived. It is this awareness alone that remains our true friend and ally upon the path. Here is why:

As long as we are willing to remain within the emerging radiance of newly dawning awareness within us, this Light in the darkness of ourselves will not allow us to fall back to spiritual sleep. This higher self-awareness is the light force that facilitates the necessary reversal or "turning around" of the two distinct natures living within us. In its presence, the formerly active parts of our lower self are made passive, and the higher aspects of us are revealed and become active. With this one great principle and practice of the true path alive in our mind, we cannot go wrong. In its gentle and corrective light, even our spiritual "mistakes" will prove themselves eventually to be in our favor. All of which brings us to this simple but perfect truth . . . so simple, virtually no one sees it, and so perfect, it dispenses justice fairly to all. I'll state it several ways.

We become what we love. What we put first in our lives is what we receive from life. The treasure of our heart both measures and determines our wealth, or our inner poverty. But not everything we love in life loves us back. Not everything we serve serves us as we imagine. Only God, only Truth, never fails us . . . never. Which brings us to the exercise that, just as the Truth it reveals, is simplicity itself.

Whenever we find ourselves confused, depressed, angry with someone, or upset with ourselves for whatever reasons, we must come wide awake and realize—through our inner awareness—that we suffer as we do because we are ruled in these moments by our own thoughts and feelings. We must see clearly that this self that dominates the moment may be doing all that it knows to do to "make the crooked places straight," but that as it is, it is just not enough. What we really need is a new and greater ruling power at work in our life than we know how to supply for ourselves. There must be no mistake about this understanding.

As the truth of our situation becomes clear—that our experience is what we are, no more, no less—we can begin simply to release ourselves, to let go of what we want and of how we think things should be. And, within this same internal movement, we can find a silent voice to call upon the Almighty with this simple request: Please step in and rule this moment.

This practicing of the presence of a power beyond our present self places us in a new relationship within ourselves. By working to remember ourselves and our God in this fashion, we agree to forget our former relationship with who we have been and its legion of impossible demands. In essence we agree to a new order within ourselves that is *for* us in a new way; we agree to have a new "first" within us. And as this inner agreement becomes established—through our willingness to put God's life before all of our other concerns—we will find that God, in turn, places us where troubles can no longer touch us.

thirteen

Encouraging Facts About Finding and Following the True Spiritual Path

To be human is to seek . . . and like small children invited to search the prepared grounds of a deluxe Easter egg hunt, every man and woman gets to find something. Just being human guarantees that. But for some seekers, collecting brightly colored things is not enough. And no matter how many prizes they find to fill their dream-lined baskets, something . . . somewhere . . . remains empty. Maybe you already know this story?

Certainly the life stories of the two people about to be introduced will at least seem familiar to you—maybe more than that. But even if not, sometimes stories such as the two that follow help shed healing light on certain parts of ourselves that may have been kept from our spiritual sight by yet other parts of us that thrive only as long as they remain in the dark. So let's turn on the light and look! Here is our first story.

In his heart, Kris knew that what had just happened to him was more luck than anything else. He had just closed the deal of a lifetime! Nevertheless, during the few seconds it took to place his "good news" call to his office coworkers, he had already cooked up a great story, working out a way to say—without really saying it—just how pivotal his personal efforts were in this great turn of fortune.

Three minutes later, even as he finishes his call, having heard all the praise his heart had hoped for, it is now a vague anxiety that calls for him.

Was that the sound of skepticism in Bill's voice? And didn't Denise seem a bit annoyed with him, challenging his version of the success story? Oh well, he would straighten up the loose ends later. The long-awaited hour had come to purchase his dream car, and nothing was going to stand in the way of this moment.

Two hours later, driving home in his new state-of-the-art automobile, Kris couldn't help but notice that as pleased as he was feeling about his new car, he sure wished he had ordered leather instead of cloth seats. And perhaps he should have insisted on the larger engine, in spite of the fuel tax. Can they tint the windows after the car leaves the factory? He also notices, too late, that he just drove right past his own off-ramp!

By the time Kris pulls into his driveway and walks up to the front door, his list of items to be changed about the car is greater than his ability to remember them. So, "naturally," when his wife smiles and asks how his day went, he immediately gets angry with her for breaking into his important line of thought—not to mention that all the evidence she needs about his day is sitting right out there in the driveway. If only she would just learn to be a little more attentive!

A few tense hours later, during what should have been a relaxed celebration dinner, his own thoughts so dominate him that he has to ask his wife to repeat what she has said several times. And later that evening, sitting alone in his favorite chair and reviewing the day's events, Kris finds himself feeling worried about the coming day. He is unsure of what is to come and already exhausted just thinking about all the fires he must either tend to or try to put out if he wants to stay on top.

Finally, just before falling into the merciful hands of sleep, he hears that all-too-familiar voice in his head ask him, as it always does on nights such as these, "How long can you keep this up? When is enough . . . enough?"

Now, let's look at our second story.

"This is a *great* party," she had to keep telling herself. "After all, what's not to like about it? It is in my honor!" Nevertheless, Tiana still couldn't shake the feeling that she wasn't the only partygoer wishing to be somewhere else at the moment—mostly because she sensed that many (if not all) of the people there felt as though the party ought not be for her, but should be for someone more worthy . . . like them!

"No," Tiana silently rebuked herself. "Let's not stoop to their level." So she probed her own heart for something less critical of others, and more truthful about herself. A slightly wry smile claimed her lips, acknowledging her finding. "Yes, that's it." Her smile broadened. The truth is that even she didn't care that she had just been named to the Board of Directors of the most prestigious charity in the region.

Imagine! For years Tiana had longed for just this moment, for her efforts to be recognized. But now, more than anything else, she was wishing the party would come to an end . . . along with this one irritating thought that kept popping, uninvited, into her mind: "Are we having fun yet?" It taunted her, even as she watched herself pretending that she was having fun. But a certain part of her enjoyed the secretly spoken sarcasm. It made her feel subtly elite, some-how better than the rest.

The sharp kick in her side from her seven-month-old fetus interrupted her daydream, bringing her abruptly back into the room. This was to be her second child, so Tiana knew there was no cause for alarm. "Thanks a lot!" she said under her breath, half kidding, half serious—knowing that her mind had carried her away to a place in herself where she didn't really like to be.

Just then she looked up to see her husband walking over toward her. She was proud of him—the way he looked, how he carried himself. Even her most cynical friends confessed how lucky she was to have found such a good man. Not only had he never hurt her, but here was someone who gave her all that he could to make her happy. They had a beautiful home, nice belongings, and even rainy-day money. "What more could you ask for?" she asked herself as she inventoried her life in the ten seconds it took for him to reach her side.

"Happy, honey?" he asked, beaming with obvious pride and confident he knew her answer.

"Oh, yes," she smiled back. "Who wouldn't be?" And then she looked away. She didn't want his searching eyes to see the lie behind her own because, if he saw that much, he might also hear what her own heart was asking her with each growing, discontented beat: "Isn't there more to life than this?"

Kris and Tiana's stories are certainly different, and yet . . . they are strangely the same.

Here we have just met two individuals striving for personal success and happiness, each traveling separate roads—paths through life that will likely never cross—yet both of which have mysteriously brought their wanderers to an identical inner moment: a point in their lives where, though worlds apart, they stand together in the very same place. Each one knows they have almost exhausted life's storehouse, and yet still finds themselves feeling incomplete within it. Which brings us to a great mystery about finding and following the true spiritual path.

Kris and Tiana may not know it just yet, but Life itself has secretly paved their way to this special inner place in which they find themselves. For in their shared moment of realizing, yet once again, that their heart's contentment is still out of sight, something else is revealed to them that is totally unexpected—something which neither has ever seen before in their walk through life.

Before their inner eyes appears another way. An unknown fork in the path of their lives emerges where once there was only one way to go. And just beyond its open and beckoning gateway can be seen the faint promise of a whole new life-possibility.

Yes, here is another mystery, hidden within the first. For this is the moment where, for each of them, their unresolved ache over all that has been begins to show itself as also being the secret seed of all that can be. They stand before the gateway to the fifth season of life . . . an invisible invitation to walk the spiritual path that leads to the Timeless Life. And for those of us who wish to understand something of this fifth season in life, to enter into it and realize the Life it leads to, we need first discover the secret seasons that reside right within our four earthly seasons.

Hidden within the nature of each of the four greater seasons—winter, spring, summer, and fall—dwells the seed of an ancient and essential life mystery, one that is as much a part of each season's unique beauty as is its obvious eternal expression.

For instance . . . look at winter, with its often white and leafless life. But even in this bleakness, something more than just its stillness speaks to us. And what we hear, if we have the ears, is more in what is not stated, for the death mask of winter also speaks of the living season to come. This unspoken spring is the mystery of winter just as a sun ray piercing a darkened sky makes the storm clouds appear even more suspenseful by revealing that something else stirs behind them.

The unmistakable signs that herald the beginning of spring hold their mystery, too. Each burgeoning bud, every green spike emerging from the dark earth, draws us into wonder at what is awakening. And wherever there is this sense of awakening, within it there is the stirring of hope, the hint of a promise yet to be fulfilled. Such is the unspoken mystery of spring. Something in us is renewed in our own embrace of life renewing itself around us. And this is how it should be. The expression of all that we see reveals everything that we don't. And what is not seen stirs in us the promise of something greater to come. The words of poet William Blake take us deeper into this mystery:

> To see a world in a grain of sand
> And a heaven in a wild flower
> Hold infinity in the palm of your hand
> And eternity in an hour.

We are rightly moved by what this higher view of life suggests is the hidden nature of reality: that whatever world we may hold before our eyes has dwelling within it another world . . . and within that one, yet another world, and another. It's true. All that we see tells us that we haven't seen it all, but that the All is right before our eyes.

The important lesson to gather here is that everything about the world around us, as well as that life within us, is in scale. To state this same idea with a slightly different slant: Within "the common" is hidden "the celestial"—as when we realize that the tiniest atom is a scale model of the solar system. This is partly what Shakespeare intended to teach when he wrote "As above, so below." And so we are about to discover that even the commonly considered four seasons of human life—our spring, summer, autumn, and winter—contain these secret realms within realms.

We begin our investigation with those more-or-less innocent days of youth, better known as the springtime of our lives. This carefree phase of life is followed soon after by the quickening heat of summer, with its fruits of love, bitter and sweet. Not long after this stage comes our autumn or fall season. These years usually mark the beginning of bittersweet dreams and wishes for softer ages past—as just down the road we can see that winter is neither far off nor will it be denied. And our lives, within the ever-whitening grip of winter, must at last reluctantly close the book on our hope of another spring.

But a deeper look into these seemingly intractable four chapters of life reveals the presence of another book hidden within this book of our lives. And written into its invisible story is a whole new chapter, complete with definite directions to a fork in the road that leads not to that full and final onset of winter, but to a permanent spring.

Here is the first part of this secret story that has been written inside of you: It begins with your discovery that each season of your individual life has within it all of the other seasons. What this means, for example, is that during your first dozen or so years, in the familiar springtime of life, you also have the experience, in scale, of a summer, fall, and winter season. But these condensed phases move through your psychic system without your awareness of them.

To help illustrate this important concept of invisible seasons playing themselves out in us, let's draw out the days of our lives, beginning with childhood. In this way we can call upon our own experience to confirm our findings. But keep in mind one important fact as we proceed: Whatever season we may study, it is safe to say that what best defines each of these life phases are those things that we hope to find within it. For instance, children seek children's things and, within each age group, the same holds true. The brief outline that follows serves simply to provide a rough example of the cycle of seasons to be found within the spring of our youth:

Spring: We dream of action figures, dolls and their houses, skateboards, three-wheeled bikes, and remote-control model cars.

Summer: In our happy hands we find those playthings that were once only dreams.

Fall: Our treasures lose their paint, their promise, and their magic as well.

Winter: Comes a boredom that would be difficult to bear if not for the hope of new and better things to come . . . which, of course, they do. In the spring-time of our youthful years it is natural for our spring to come again . . . and again . . . with each new dream that we know to dream.

But as life itself is soon to teach, this seemingly inexhaustible springtime of youth passes on. Its transition is marked by the growing realization that what we are going to need to be content is more than just toys, for we are headed into our summer season. Young, socially conscious adults no longer seek "kid stuff." Now it is the stuff of romance, sophisticated machines, and the money to have both that push their way to the front of summer's wish list.

Here again, with just a little use of our imagination, we can see in our second life season all four seasons playing out just as they did in our springtime. First, dreams of achievement, then their fulfillment . . . too soon the fading victories, followed by new battles to be fought and hopefully to be won. Around and around the seasons go within this summer until its warmth gradually fades.

Only this time around, when the winter of our summer season finally arrives—as it must—it doesn't just bring the same cooled feelings that marked the end of the spring of our youth. With it comes another kind of chill, and in it a different order of dissatisfaction enters the heart. It feels as though something is trying to break through to us from within us . . . and it is.

For, poised right between this undeniable winter of our summer season and the incoming spring of our approaching fall, there appears a fifth season—a new time within the cycle of life that originates from far beyond it. But please note: Regardless of what name we give to this extraordinary life phase, it is vital not to confuse its temporary appearance with the usual unhappiness that weaves its way through the regular seasons of our lives. This season of divine discontent and those recurring phases of everyday sadness and disappointment have nothing in common. This fifth season of life is unique because of what grows in its time: a gradually all-encompassing new wish for a relationship with something that never passes away.

It is here, in this first true spiritual season, that we are given the eyes to see that what we had been seeking throughout all our seasons past is powerless to satisfy us. This insight is the first fruit. The second fruit of this spiritual season is the sweet discovery that we have no reason to fear our new findings.

In this time of inner awakening, the truth dawns upon us that our contentment in each of our previous life seasons had to be as momentary as were those temporary things we knew to seek out within them. And though painful to our self-pictures of being the great provider, it is also abundantly clear that we need more than we know how to give ourselves. We have finally learned that the brightly colored Easter eggs, which once thrilled us and kept us seeking more to fill our dream-lined basket through the seasons of our life, disappear as fast as we collect them. What we really want from our lives isn't a way to have more of what is new, but a Way *to be* New, to be Real, to be Permanent. And now everything is in place for this to happen. Our newly awakened divine discontent promises to keep us from falling back to sleep and slipping back into those bittersweet dreams of better seasons to come. In its light we can see the entrance to a new world within the old one . . . the gateway to the true spiritual path.

The Right Wish and Real Work for Awakening

It feels like I have been a seeker forever, but have not yet found the enlightenment I have been seeking. Is enlightenment something that happens, or is it just an understanding?

Try not to make so much out of the idea of enlightenment. Awakening is in scale, and to answer your question, it is instantaneous understanding. For instance, every time you can catch "you" about to defeat you, this glimpse into your own inner workings is a form of enlightenment. Why? Because what was formerly in the dark now has light. Instantly your suffering is diminished. As a person begins to prefer this inner light to the false sense of self that inner darkness produces, it follows (in the wake of this new understanding) that what is untrue must perish. This is the true beginning of dying to ourselves. So it follows: We awaken first in order to die, and as we die to ourselves, there is a rebirth. Ultimately, it could be said that this rebirth, this fully established Light in a man or a woman, is what it means to be "enlightened."

If we ask for the truth and really wish to have it, will we receive it? Truth is not denied anyone who really wants it, is it?

In the Koran, Mohammed said something to this effect: "Put your faith in Allah, but tie up your camel." We know this saying as "God helps those who help themselves." Our wish for God/Truth is the beginning, but we must be willing to make the inner journey. If, in your wish for the life of Truth, you will just put one foot down in front of the next while keeping your eye on the mark, you can be assured that everything you need to succeed will be provided.

So many people speak today of the idea of self-development and the idea of working on themselves. What does it mean to develop the self? Is this really possible to do?

True spiritual self-development does not mean struggling to improve the self but rather to transcend its limited levels through self-observation. The task is not to become something new, but to see through the parts of ourselves that stand between us and the new life that already exists within us as unrealized spiritual potential. It might be better said that self-development is the stretch of country we walk between the old world of what we have been and the new world we enter into when realizing the still, secret Self within.

It would seem that every time I set out to make myself a more loving person, I succeed at first, but soon forget all about this compassionate person I want to be and am back to being my usual, detached self. What can't I see here?

Don't set out to be a loving person. Not only is this not the goal, but it is unattainable for the self that seeks it. A rose never sets out to be fragrant. Its perfume is already a part of its natural nature that only needs certain conditions in order to be expressed. Making an aim without understanding the real target must result in missing the mark. The corrective inner action to take is to wake up to what stands unconsciously between you and the natural state of compassion, humility, and meekness you are created to express. The right order is to try to see, not try to be. In this new kind of seeing will come the being and the love you are longing for.

I know something great waits for me somewhere, but I haven't a clue what it is or how to actualize it. How do I find what I really want from this life?

In the East there is an expression used to describe both the way one finds the true spiritual path and how to stay upon this invisible course. Translated, the words mean "Not this, not that." In other words, we come upon what is true, what alone can fill the empty place in our heart, by awakening to what doesn't work, and then walking away from that—whatever "that" may be. This is the path of negation. When we know what is false for us, then we are that much closer to coming upon what is true.

Working For the Awakening You Long For

There are two things I have learned: Be true to myself and live in the moment. Will this be enough?

Being true to one's self and working to be aware of one's self in the moment is, more or less, the alpha and the omega of all spiritual work. Within it is born integrity, humility, and compassion. Buddha called this Way "dharma." Continue on this celestial course and allow Truth to make its corrections as it will.

I have had moments of spiritual awakening. Yet these moments seem to fade all too quickly. When such moments arise, I have a new depth of clarity and silence. Are there any specific lessons to apply during these moments to help anchor myself there?

Nothing is more priceless than those moments when we suddenly are able to see that the world we took as being everything was only a small part of a greater something. Suddenly, we realize we indeed dwell within ourselves within a much larger world than we could have hoped existed. When these awakenings come, it seems natural to want to hang onto them, but consider the following: In a certain sense, that moment of Light came unannounced. Its presence awakened you to itself and all that it revealed. Now "you" want to be the one who possesses this Light and who can call upon it at will. This "you" is what is standing between you and the Light and, as difficult as it is to do, you must work at letting go of every wish you have to return to any moment once glimpsed.

It is clear to me that I can't just wait and see if my life will get better, but looking into myself seems to pull me down. Do you have any leg-up advice for me?

Always remember these two ideas, and they will become your personal friends, dedicated to helping you fulfill your wish to be free: First—there is always something higher. This means that regardless of what you may see within you, just above it is a place of new power and purpose that you can touch simply by remembering that it always and already exists. And second, connected to this first idea, there is no such thing as a fact you can find out *about* yourself that is not *for* yourself.

As sincere seekers of self-realization, what can we do to bring ourselves the most spiritual gold?

Here are five steps to new spiritual riches: (1) Walk in the direction of what you fear losing the most. (2) Put the love of truth before the fear of being without everyone and everything. (3) Never talk to yourself about what you see within yourself. (4) Never justify what you want to talk to yourself about. (5) Refuse to blame anyone else for what you see within yourself. Take these deliberate steps, and watch how your pockets fill with real spiritual wealth.

Is real happiness actually effortless? The inner work I know is needed seems to be a constant struggle.

Don't confuse the work to cultivate the soil with the garden that grows in the prepared soil. Real happiness is indeed effortless, once the causes of unhappiness are weeded out. In a way, you already know this truth through the experience of those moments where your joy is independent of the "you" that suddenly realizes it is having a happy time. This physical example can be applied to our spiritual life when we come to the new contentment born out of seeing that our former discontentment was rooted in a lie. Don't struggle to make yourself happy. Persist instead with your efforts to be free of the illusion that you must somehow struggle with unhappy thoughts or feelings. See these dark states as passing clouds. As you do this, you will know that behind them sits the sun.

Use the Ground of Discovery
to Realize Your Self

If we wish to realize the Real Life that only a life of truth can provide, we must each agree not only to put truth first in our lives, but to will this highest of intentions every day with all we can gather within ourselves to do so. There are no shortcuts to reaching this higher ground in us. However, we may be rightly encouraged to know that there is no substitute for the naturally prevailing sense of peace and harmony that attends this inner world, much in the same way as warmth and light surround our great sun.

The encouragement we need to proceed with our quest is all around us . . . hidden in some ways, and yet present in plain view for those whose inner eyes have begun to open. Take, for instance, what happens to us inwardly when we round a bend and see before our eyes a pasture of sun-brightened flowers. In this moment, the emerging array of delicate colors slowly fills our senses and we are drawn into its community.

Drawing nearer still in our approach, our consciousness increasingly takes in this pastoral realm, and even as it enters into us, do we enter into it. But consider herein the following truth: We neither create the beauty of this moment nor the consciousness now absorbed within it. The whole of this relationship already exists or else it could not have become part of our experience. This beautiful idea reveals the truth of how our exterior world of experience provides for us a special kind of mirror in which it is not only possible to see ourselves, but to enter consciously into these deep, undetected realms of our True Self.

It is impossible to enter into something that doesn't have prior existence, just as nothing that exists could enter into us unless its existence were already a part of our consciousness. Now, with this truth in your mind, substitute the idea of the field of flowers that we approach for the principle of higher understanding, of Truth. What do you see? What have we discovered here?

It is not we who grow in understanding, in the light, any more than that field of flowers grows as we approach it from around a bend. The field was already present, with all its forms and colors, only awaiting a fortunate discoverer. This exact same principle holds true for the presence of higher understanding and those truths by which we approach it. This Wisdom is already flowered and awaits only a special wanderer to enter its private domain. This interior Ground of all that may be discovered belongs to anyone and everyone who will do the work needed to realize it. No one owns this Ground, yet we may each possess as much of it as we are willing to exchange our lives for. Everyone has the same right to the deep riches of these eternal essences. And any spiritual seeds planted within them grow equally for whosoever will stoop to plant them.

The great Sun above this Ground never stops shining, so that there is Light enough everywhere in all times for all its creations to develop and grow. These things I tell you are intended to convey this one truth: The true spiritual life cannot be separated from the ground of discovery out of which it springs, and through which it lives. For us, for now, they are one thing. And this finding brings us face to face with one inescapable fact: This ground of discovery, the Ground of God's life, remains little more than earthly dirt for us unless we dive into it and are willing to get our hands dirty. Only then are we made clean. The confusions and doubts inherent in merely speculating about the spiritual life are washed away by our honest spiritual sweat.

But there is more to this metaphor. To succeed spiritually, to discover the new man or woman waiting within us, requires going beyond being the thought-based, self-conceived creatures we are at present. We must work on ourselves. Only honest self-work heals the unconscious divisions within us and between us.

Imagine two people working the earth. Side by side they till the ground beneath them. Both know the quality of the soil, its weeds and rocks, and the heat of the overhead sun as it bears down upon them. There is no argument between them about the nature of the ground they cultivate.

Neither person at work finds it necessary to have or hold some belief about the earth beneath their feet—or about what it can, or can't, do for them. Why? Because *they stand upon it.* They are in it. They can taste it in the very air they breathe. Each person shares the work and receives the rewards of his or her efforts.

One way that we can start working upon the ground of discovery is to stop speculating about the nature of truth. We can dare to see that our beliefs about what is assumed true are worse than worthless if, because of them, we have found a way to justify self-righteousness, indolence, cruelty, or any other self-isolating, negative state of mind.

The merely mental person has no idea that his endless confusion can never be resolved by the equally endless questions he formulates to escape it . . . that these same questions are merely secret extensions of the very states from which he suffers. Where, then, is the answer to be found? We must know the truth of ourselves, for in this Truth are all other truths hidden. "But how?" you might ask.

There is only one real answer to this question. *Be real.* Live what you are *now*—in this moment and in every other moment. Watch life within you without resistance to what you see. To be real is to realize the reality of our selves, whatever that may be in the moment.

And again you might ask, "But how?"

Each time life finds you without a clue, stop supplying yourself with answers you *think* you know. Instead, stand upon the ground of that moment. Dig there! Enter into the ground of discovery now at your feet. Consciously work these virgin soils and watch how new life begins to root and grow.

As we grow to understand that the ground of discovery, along with its hard work and priceless rewards, is always right beneath our feet wherever we are, whatever we may be doing, we realize that there is never a moment wherein we can't be cultivating our relationship with Truth.

Add to this truth the fact that the only real change that can occur in the conditions we call our life must begin with a change in our consciousness, and there is only one course of action remaining. We must agree to enter into the ground of discovery, embrace our findings there, and go to work on what we uncover! If we will do our part, the Truth will take care of the rest. What grows from our efforts will never falter or fail us.

fourteen

Keys to Completing the Journey to Your Self

Outside the closed gates, and leading into the spacious, outdoor entrance area of the School for Higher Learning, stood a small, somewhat anxious group of a few dozen truth seekers. Each was waiting for the much-anticipated moment of greeting and then being tested by the school's master—a man known the world over for his perfected wisdom and ability to help others gain the same.

Nervous chatter filled the air. Everyone there already understood, going in, that only a very few select students were accepted, even though none standing there outside the school's walls knew the real reasons why. And to make matters even more tense, every ten minutes or so the school gates would open and out would march three or four student-candidates, mumbling to themselves in not too hushed, angry tones. The crowd of waiting would-be students couldn't help but overhear the comments.

"Who are they kidding?"

"I knew I shouldn't have come!"

"No one can do that!"

"This teacher's a fake; he asks the impossible!"

And even as the disgruntled students stormed off, another band of seekers was invited in to be tested.

The small group admitted this time numbered five. And the last two through the gate, before it closed, were a young married couple. They were shaky, but determined. There was much at stake for them. After all, it was only a few short months before that they had confessed to themselves (and to each other) that the world, taken on its own terms, was an empty place. They had agreed there had to be more, and it was in their hearts to find this "something" higher. Perhaps this school for Truth would show them the Way.

But a moment later, their hopes came crashing down. Their own groans and moans echoed the disbelief of their fellow contestants as they stared, mouths hung open, at what now stood between them and their dream.

Just before them, like something out of the land of the giants, stood what appeared to be a towering, whitewashed high-hurdle whose top bar had to be at least twenty feet above the ground! A large hand-lettered sign was nailed to one of its two supporting uprights. It read:

> No one permitted past this point! To win entrance into this School for Higher Learning, this hurdle

must be cleared using nothing other than your
own strength.

And, as if these instructions weren't impossible enough,
the last line on the sign was the final straw:

No ladders or poles allowed. Only one attempt
permitted!

It took less than ten seconds for the five people in the
group to see they were sunk. And even less time elapsed
before all manner of heated comments and complaints started flying around—exactly like those they had heard only
minutes before when they stood outside the school's gates
waiting their turn to be tested.

En masse the newly defeated group of seekers turned on
their heels and marched out, carrying the young married
couple along with them like a dust devil captures small
leaves. Neither he nor she knew what was happening to them
until, a few miles farther down the road, the energy of the
storm that had picked them up, dropped them off . . . leaving
them on their own and alone again.

After sitting there awhile, stunned at the events of the day
and examining their own hearts, they looked deeply into
each other's eyes. It was decision time. Do they give up their
search? Return to their old lives? Just hope that things will
work out? Or do they attempt the unthinkable? Should they
swallow their pride and return to the school for Truth to
plead for an interview with the master, and somehow learn
the secret of how to get over the impossibly high hurdle?

A brief moment later they were headed back up the road
toward the school.

When they arrived at the front entrance area, not a single soul was left in line. They had figured this would be so by the number of angry seekers they had seen surging past them moving in the opposite direction. But this time, instead of being shut, the gates were open, so the two of them just walked in.

Again the impossibly high hurdle stood before them. And though there was no way to say for sure, it looked as though the high bar was even higher than they remembered. But so what? Nowhere was anyone to be seen. The woman spoke out, breaking the silence of the yard: "Hello! Anybody around?" Only stillness answered.

The young man took his sweetheart's hand. Together they took a deep breath. And then, collecting themselves as best they could, they walked right under the high hurdle, past the sign reading *No one permitted without first clearing the high hurdle*, and entered the school. This time the man spoke up politely, but with resolve: "Hello! We're here to see the teacher . . . please?"

A kind voice followed so closely on the heels of his own that it made both of them jump:

"And what do you wish with the teacher?"

"We want to learn how to get over that impossibly high hurdle that stands just outside there," said the young man, pointing back through the doors they had come through. Then he put his arm around his wife, and drawing her nearer, he continued speaking. "Please, sir, we want to pass the test you've designed, even though we know we can't. Isn't there something . . . some way . . . ?" His eyes, meeting the eyes of the teacher, finished his thought for him. Then the young man returned his gaze to his wife. They smiled at one another, accepting their defeat. How could they know that what they were about to hear the next moment would shake the smile from their faces?

"But you've already passed the test," spoke the teacher. "You're welcome to stay here, to learn all that you can."

The thought in the young man's mind was yelling "What?!" but thankfully it was his voice, shaking somewhat, that said quietly, "But I don't understand. We failed to even take your test, let alone pass it!"

"Oh no," the master smiled back at them, knowing they didn't yet understand what was taking place. "You only failed the test that you *thought* was the test," and his smile broadened, "which isn't the real test at all." He indicated they should follow him outside to the courtyard test-site area and, as he talked, together they walked out into the sunlight.

"In the higher life you seek, there are many obstacles to success . . . some great, some small. But there is one hurdle that stands as a sentinel before all real inner growth, barring the unprepared seeker from entering the Real Life. This highest of hurdles is what we *think* we already know about this path of ourselves. This false certainty, along with its remorseless shadow—pride—keeps us from being able to learn those truths we need to know."

He looked directly at them to ensure his next point wouldn't be missed, and paused to indicate a special lesson was about to be imparted. "So you see, to be able to get over this high hurdle takes a special kind of spirit . . . it takes one that is willing to walk under this bar."

Looking at them once again, to be sure they understood the inner meaning of his words, he finished his thought as he politely excused himself and walked away. "Which is why the two of you are now welcome! May your studies here be fruitful." And with those words, he turned the corner and was gone.

Finding Freedom from Weariness and Frustration

It seems that the more aware I become and the more I am able to see, my thoughts increase in number and speed. Some days I am so weary that it feels like I need a holiday from awareness. Is it possible to overdo it?

Ask yourself, does the sunlight need a break from the nighttime, or do these two powers naturally rotate with no conflict? Anything that tries to tell you that you need a break from being aware belongs to the self that would rather sleep through life than live.

The struggle to stay awake sometimes feels like a wrestling match with myself in which I'm badly overmatched and getting thrown out of the ring on a daily basis. How can I get on top and stay there?

Wrestle on! Don't be concerned with the outcome, and don't worry about who is on top. You have heard that "the battle has already been won." I assure you, it is true. We must volunteer and be willing to endure whatever we must in order to eventually come to the realization that there is nothing we must endure. It is one of those paradoxes. But, if we will just stay in the ring of reality, oh, what a prize!

Some mornings when I sit down for my quiet time to meditate or pray, instead of peace reigning in me, it's a

mental pounding that rains down on me. Then I feel powerless or begin blaming myself for not doing it "right." I wind up feeling this great sense of loss, as though I have been cheated by God and I am a hopeless case. What's happening to me?

This is an important stage of your work. I know it is difficult to understand, but your awareness of all the conflicting thoughts and feelings is your reward for your efforts. The first thing that all of us who are working to become new men and women must remember is that virtually nothing within us is actually interested in this transformation. It is difficult to work against the great and often overpowering inner shadows, such as feeling worthless or powerless whenever we make a new aim for ourselves. But the pressure of negative states such as you have described is often the indication that what we are attempting to do is the right and true course for us. Any interior voices that tell you either how illuminated or dark you are, are part of what must be released, not embraced. Dare to stand alone with your wish for Truth only. It will stand with you when you do this.

When I stop and think about all the things that I feel I must do in order to grow spiritually, I start to feel so discouraged. Isn't there a simpler approach to self-liberation?

One of the earliest and most important lessons that each of us must embrace (and embrace over and over again) is to learn what it means to work with what is in our power and not be overtaken by trying to deal with what is not in our power. For instance, it is not in your power to make flooding emotions settle down by any form of resistance to them or by wishing them to go away. What *is* in your power is to recognize that any dark emotion only has the power that you lend to it through not recognizing it for what it is: an impostor self that seeks to draw you into its circle of influence in order to keep you going in circles. Drop all feelings of yourself that seem to tell you discouraging things about yourself. They are not real, and neither is the "you" that would struggle with them.

> **Whenever I read truthful writings or hear wisdom spoken, I feel a certain excitement like nothing else I have ever felt before. But in what seems like no time at all, I cool off and even forget how excited I was about working along the path to freedom. Is this condition a natural one?**

As strange as it sounds, it is natural at times to lose our zeal for awakening. This sense of self-loss is actually a necessary step along the higher path. For many years a person can work for greater wholeness, for a spiritual life, based on a partially unconscious desire to fulfill themselves with the image and the requisite feelings that attend such thoughts. Again, this is a natural progression. But as we work, this self and its desires will naturally fade, and with it seems to go our zeal for self-work. This is where it gets interesting. It is only when we persist along the path, in spite of our lukewarm emotions, that we begin to realize there has been something within us doing the work all along, and that it will continue to do so if we will simply allow it to. As this self-discovery grows, our faith becomes real in proportion to our realization of just how true this finding actually is. There is an Intelligence at work for us, within us, that wants more for us than we do for ourselves.

The True Measure of Spiritual Growth

I think that I am on the road to enlightenment, but my thoughts would lead me to believe that only the holiest of holies could ever reach that state, and it is not readily achievable to a parent having to work and raise a family. How do I recognize my progress?

While it is true the awakened life that attends self-realization may not be for the masses, nothing about this truth precludes the possibility of a good householder establishing a relationship with God/Truth. Anyone who would have you believe that a good, innocent, and holy life is beyond your reach is himself out of touch with reality. Life places each and every one of us in precisely the conditions we need to learn the lessons required for our awakening. Covet no one else's life. Work to uncover the truth that awaits you within your own. And as far as how to recognize your progress is concerned, don't look for growth. When we actually do change our nature, one of the first changes in us is that we are freed from thinking about ourselves at all in terms of being "better" or "worse."

As I learn more about higher ideas, I find moments of great clarity and understanding. Yet, at times, the progress I seem to have made in one area or another seems to get attacked even harder by yet some other negativity I didn't suspect was there in me. Is there an explanation for these events?

Here is some real encouragement: Everything about this Work is already established with laws that, once understood, guarantee inner success. For instance, be assured that all moments of spiritual grace or new insight will be followed by visitations from opposing forces. For instance, Satan was at the Last Supper; hence the old, truthful saying, "The greater the light, the greater the darkness." The problem is not that these opposing forces consistently appear, but that they find someone willing to identify with their presence and purpose.

Is it possible for certain unconscious parts of a person to make him believe he is making spiritual progress when he is actually not?

Of course. These deceptive parts of ourselves are virtually always at work. But more to the point, and perhaps more helpful, is to understand that our real progress in the spiritual life is freedom from the need to measure ourselves at all. What we are after with our inner work is release from this comparative-thought self, not to find a way to confirm ourselves with it. And as this understanding grows clearer, it becomes impossible for us to be tricked.

The more intensely I work to apply truthful ideas and to realize their power, the more my own mind throws negative images at me, such as how powerless I am to win such a high undertaking. How does one know whether their inner condition is actually improving or secretly getting worse?

Keep your eye on your aim, not on those parts of you telling you that you have missed the mark. The feeling that one's condition is worsening is a natural and somewhat expected effect of the intimate enemy doing what it can to keep you in its dark stronghold. These states of siege are a sure sign of a person's inner progress, even though it feels just the opposite. In a way, it could be said that the devil always defeats himself this way, by showing his hand. So don't stop. Press forward. Continue with your studies. If you will persist, these attacks will reveal themselves to be the empty forces they have always been.

Learning to Let Go

What exactly does it mean to "let go," and how do I begin to do this with pervasive negative states, such as my anger?

Each of us has a special kind of free will, only we don't understand it and, more significantly, we don't know what it is for. Attention is a kind of special energy that connects an individual to what he holds in his mind. Working to be awake reveals where our attention is. And as we realize that we suffer the way we do because we are unconscious of where our attention has gone without us—for instance, being on angry thoughts all the time—then choosing to let go of this unseen attachment becomes natural and effortless.

If seeing and letting go of what is false is a means to what is true, is departing from what one doesn't love a means of arriving at what one loves?

Yes. It is quite a mystery. Solving it requires that we begin to see how certain conditions in our lives (that we "love") themselves hold us and our wish for a higher, happier life in contempt. So it is here that the path of negation can be a good guide. Knowing what we no longer want in our lives, and working to drop it, creates both the space for the new to reveal itself as well as to help weaken the grip of those parts of ourselves clinging to what is self-limiting and secretly self-destructive.

Every time I get close to mental quiet, I experience a fearful reflex reaction. Though this quiet sensation is indescribably pleasant, my reaction comes on so fast and strong that I feel as though I am being sucked down a black hole. Do you have any insights into this condition and how I might go past it?

Your experience is not unknown. There are many parts in us that are literally terrified of this letting go as you have described it. The reason is that our present self only knows itself by what it considers, or by what opposes it. When we let go, what we are really doing is consciously negating this self that is a creation of the opposites. As your understanding increases as to the mechanical operation of this level of self, you will be able to step back from its projected fears and let go in greater and greater measure. Keep testing the waters. When we ask for something higher, and we are sincere in this request, that wish cannot be denied. Fear of the unknown is the way darkness obstructs the arrival of a condition within us in which fear cannot dwell. Understand this. Let go.

How is letting go of ourselves different from waking up to ourselves?

These two states of self go hand in hand and, while different, are still a part of each other. The mind tends to always perceive things by cause and effect. Letting go of ourselves comes in direct proportion to what we see is no longer tenable about us within us. As this natural shedding of self takes place, what formerly filled this space within us is replaced with a new and higher order of energy that, relative to our former self, is decidedly more aware and attentive . . . hence, more awake. Step by step, we succeed in this way.

Special Insights into Making a Fresh Start in Life

I sense a need in myself to step up the intensity of my spiritual work, but this "sensing" normally follows my realization that I am quite lazy and comfortable where I am. Is there a way to wake up to what I need to do next rather than to merely react in disgust at my own lack of direction?

We cannot help but increase our inner efforts as it becomes clear to us that our spiritual sleep is driving us nowhere—that is to say except deeper into dependency with unseen, downward-sliding parts of ourselves. No man or woman will consciously let themselves degenerate. Stay aware of the nature whose tendency it is to always take the easy way through life, and your wish to rise above it will increase incrementally. The wish will do the rest.

What must we do to reach a higher level of ourselves?

Life itself is always offering us the answers we need. For instance, nature abhors a vacuum. This means that wherever a vacuum exists, nature will flood in to fill it. Apply this practical knowledge to your spiritual life. When we won't follow the usual thoughts and feelings, a kind of vacuum occurs. Usually the pressure of this pushes us to fill the space with what is familiar (i.e., with what we know or think we know will work for us). But when we will place higher principles before the longing we have to know ourselves in a familiar way, and not give ourselves the comfort of our own answers, in flows a new and higher understanding. Take this knowledge and work with it.

Working to be more inwardly observant of myself has brought about invaluable changes in all areas of my life. However, just recently, I feel stuck in a comfort zone where I don't want to do the work of seeing more of myself. How do I get going again?

This may help: Once you have become as inwardly quiet as possible, ask sincerely for God to show you exactly what you need to see about yourself. When you make this wish, make it fully. Work as best you can to be conscious of what it is like to remain you. This kind of honest inner seeing not only creates true incentive for self-change, but provides the new ground you need in yourself to continue your growth. The untold great spiritual secret concerning self-transformation is that we grow in proportion to our awareness of what we can no longer be.

Each morning I have asked for something new and true to be shown to me. I have been surprised by what has been given to me. Some of it, for the moment, has been painful. At other times, it has been joyful. It is always surprising. The upshot of it is, "Why, of course. How could I have not seen it before?"

One of the most exciting aspects of real self-work is that as we become new, so do our moments. Our awakened nature never experiences repetition, which means every moment has a new taste to it. Even our so-called bad moments are new, because they bring with them new lessons to learn about ourselves. With persistence on your part, it will be a new world that will wake you up every morning. I promise that these words are not an affirmation, but a fact of the higher life that awaits all who will ask for it.

Find Freedom from False Beliefs
and Their False gods

The work of liberating ourselves begins in an unlikely place not dissimilar to a small spring that bubbles up in the heart of a deep desert. Its pure, emerging waters bring life a chance to flourish there in the midst of all the dry sands around it. And so it is that from somewhere deep within each of us springs the need to be true, whole, and free. But even as these spiritual waters rise to the surface in us, refreshing our wish for unconditional freedom, they encounter either the heated nature of some smoldering desire or its rocklike residue in the hardened form of a conditioned thought. Spirit and matter meet, expanding and constricting primordial opposites collide, and we are their ground. These truths are self-evident if we care to see them, and their discovery sets the stage for the task before us.

First, we must come to understand what happens within us and to us in each moment when these fresh and pure upwelling spiritual impulses encounter this inbred, downward-trending captive nature called the false self. In particular, we must see how the mechanical longings of our lower self don't so much swallow up this living wish to be free as they secretly misdirect it—sending us off in the search for what promises to quench our thirst, but that secretly serves to enflame it. This one spiritually significant insight helps explain why we must place this work of self-seeing ahead of all else. As long as we cling to the false belief that one desire, regardless of its nature, can free us from the unwanted effects of another one, we will remain the unconscious servants of these desires and the false gods they create to temporarily satisfy them.

Following are twenty-five widely held false beliefs. No false belief can exist without some form of false power to father it. These false powers are false gods. Our study and special exercise is to shed much-needed light into their secret hiding places. But, before we begin this important investigation, we need to establish a common understanding of certain study terms.

What is a false belief?

A false belief is any idea that holds something to be true that is not.

What is a false god?

A false god is any mental image, or idea, whose existence provides for us a false sensation of life, chiefly through its persistent and impotent promise to deliver strength, security, or lasting contentment.

What does it mean to serve a false god?

Fake gods can only deliver their own nature, which, like their own un-life, is empty of anything real and permanent. So, while these fake forces may offer you—through tempting, false beliefs such as the ones listed below—something real and lasting, all they can really provide you with is another of their empty promises and its attending heartache!

What can I expect to learn from this study?

Follow the sequence of the next four ideas closely. It is important that you think these insights through for yourself. As you permit them to show you the nature of the "powers" that drive the self through the circles holding it captive, you will also begin to see the way up and out of these psychological pitfalls:

- False beliefs create false needs.

- False needs create compulsive cravings.

- Cravings cause suffering.

- As the pain increases, we search for something with the power to deliver us from our troubles. In unseen hope and desperation, we return to that same false belief that betrayed us in the first place. Thus a false god is born—a god not only powerless to affect our rescue, but one that is actually a cause of our unremitting stress and sorrow!

What personal benefits will I realize if I practice this exercise?

All the attending stresses—those fears and furies found in your inner life—are born out of mistaking and then embracing the false life of false gods for being that of your own. You serve them only in the vain and aching hope that one day a false god will make good on its promise. This is like believing that one day a despotic government will rid itself of its own tyranny. As you eliminate false beliefs, the cycle of unnatural suffering comes to a natural close. Into its place flows real strength, unflappable composure, new compassion, and confidence, just to name a few of the prizes awarded those who see through their own false beliefs.

How can I make the most of this exercise?

For best results, consider each of these following false beliefs as a separate and personal study. For extra spiritual gold, take one at a time and, before reading it, refresh your memory with the title of this exercise: Twenty-Five False Beliefs that Keep You Serving False gods. This approach is especially helpful. It will remind you twenty-five times that the reason you are doing this special self-investigative work is to reveal something about yourself to yourself. And remember the key word here is *reveal*.

We must never forget, regardless of what we may find within ourselves, that self-revelation and spiritual elevation are two wings on the same bird. For this exercise to succeed in lifting you beyond the influences and internal injury of the false gods in your life, you must be willing to see those invisible parts of yourself that do embrace false beliefs as being true.

Lastly, it may seem that some of the false beliefs below apply to you and some don't. Or, with a few of them, you may feel it is only a question of some small degree. Whatever your reaction, be assured there is no reason to fear or otherwise resist any particular discovery. Fear is a perfect example of a false belief at work. Its premise is simple: Just believe that what you don't see can't hurt you. Sure! This is like falling off a boat at sea and closing your eyes in the water so that a lurking shark won't see you!

Remember: All false beliefs and their false gods survive only in the dark. It is important to realize that some of the false beliefs listed below are subtler then others, and that they will not readily show themselves as false. To expect a false god to stand out in the open and proclaim itself as such would be spiritually immature. On the other hand, and as a kind of perennial spiritual guideline, what is internally false usually feels compelled to claim itself true. So should you hear any internal protests while you read, simply recall a paraphrase of Shakespeare's immortal words, "Methinks thou doth protest too much!"

Twenty-Five False Beliefs that Keep You Serving False gods

- Mentally rehashing painful events is the key to resolving them.

- The faster you can go though life, the more you will accomplish.

- Anger, revenge, or resentment are only a natural and healthy response to having been wronged.

- The past is responsible for your present aching, angry state.

- There is intelligence in consensus.

- Appearing as though you are in charge of yourself is the same as self-possession.

- There is security and strength to be found in being part of a group.

- That self-pleased feeling that follows flattery is good for you.

- Life is for some and against others, so victory or defeat in life depends upon the fates.

- The more you are able to convince others of how great you are, the greater you are.

- There is no such thing as evil.

- Spiritual development is evolutionary, not voluntary, which means there is no need for inner work.

- The agreement of others with your point of view means your view is the right one.

- Other people you know are happy with themselves, as they have already found in the world the contentment you are looking for.

- Imitating the life of someone successful is the pathway to personal success.

- Tomorrow will be better!

- Those who praise you do so because you are praiseworthy.

- Being alone in life means going through life lonely.

- Anytime you want to, you can walk away from it all.

- It takes time to forgive those who have hurt you.

- Better to pretend that you understand than to let others see that you don't.

- Being able to see, or point out, where another is wrong means you are right to do so.

- Agreeing to go along with certain negative states is natural and necessary for your well-being.

- A quiet, peaceful mind is not likely to be a productive one.

- There are some areas of life where it is just impossible to start all over again.

Our wish to know the Truth of ourselves calls for us to awaken within ourselves. And as our inner eyes gradually open to the many worlds within us—with their diverse scope of thoughts, feelings, and forces (friendly and not)—we find ourselves strangers in a strange land. We discover at work in us new laws and their unseen enforcers; we realize uncountable levels of consciousness and their attending states of peace and conflict, captivity and freedom. And as our inner eyes develop and adjust themselves to see by the light illuminating this interior kingdom, we see that we are the world we would overcome.

This unthinkable glimpse takes us beyond belief, beyond the mere idea of God, and into the one life that is His . . . and now revealed to us as being our own. In the growing light of this revelation, fear, hatred, and anger begin to fall away from us because we no longer need these ancient appendages with which we once ruled our world. We are free because the Truth has shown us that the self who would be complete can never attain its desire, while the Self that already is needs only to shake, wake, and extract itself from the dream of what it is not.

☽ REACH FOR THE MOON

Llewellyn publishes hundreds of books on your favorite subjects!
To get these exciting books, including the ones on the following pages,
check your local bookstore or order them directly from Llewellyn.

Order by Phone

- Call toll-free within the U.S. and Canada, 1-800-THE MOON
- In Minnesota, call (651) 291-1970
- We accept VISA, MasterCard, and American Express

Order by Mail

- Send the full price of your order (MN residents add 7% sales tax)
  in U.S. funds, plus postage & handling to:

  Llewellyn Worldwide
  P.O. Box 64383, Dept. 0-7387-0107-6
  St. Paul, MN 55164-0383, U.S.A.

Postage & Handling

- **Standard (U.S., Mexico, & Canada):** If your order is $20.00 or under, add $5.00;
  $20.01–$100.00, add $6.00; over $100, shipping is free

(Continental U.S. orders ship UPS. AK, HI, PR, & P.O. Boxes ship USPS 1st class.
Mex. & Can. ship PMB.)

Second Day Air (Continental U.S. only): $10.00 for one book + $1.00 per each
additional book

**Express (AK, HI, & PR only) [Not available for P.O. Box delivery. For street
address delivery only.]:** $15.00 for one book + $1.00 per each additional book

International Surface Mail: Add $1.00 per item

International Airmail: Books—Add the retail price of each item;
non-book items—Add $5.00 per item

> **Please allow 4–6 weeks for delivery on all orders.**
> **Postage and handling rates subject to change.**

Discounts

We offer a 20% discount to group leaders or
agents. You must order a minimum of 5 copies of
the same book to get our special quantity price.

Free Catalog

Get a free copy of our color catalog, *New
Worlds of Mind and Spirit.* Subscribe for just
$10.00 in the United States and Canada ($30.00
overseas, airmail).

Visit our website at www.llewellyn.com for more information.

The Secret of Letting Go
Guy Finley

Whether you need to let go of a painful heartache, a destructive habit, a frightening worry, or a nagging discontent, *The Secret of Letting Go* shows you how to call upon your own hidden powers and how they can take you through and beyond any challenge or problem. This book reveals the secret source of a brand-new kind of inner strength.

In the light of your new and higher self-understanding, emotional difficulties such as loneliness, fear, anxiety, and frustration fade into nothingness as you happily discover they never really existed in the first place.

With a foreword by Desi Arnaz Jr., and introduction by Dr. Jesse Freeland, *The Secret of Letting Go* is a pleasing balance of questions and answers, illustrative examples, truth tales, and stimulating dialogues that allow the reader to share in the exciting discoveries that lead up to lasting self-liberation.

This is a book for the discriminating, intelligent, and sensitive reader who is looking for *real* answers.

0-87542-223-3; 240 pp., 5¼ x 8 $9.95

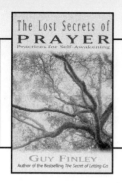

The Lost Secrets of Prayer
Practices for Self-Awakening

Guy Finley

Do your prayers go unanswered? Or when they are answered, do the results bring you only *temporary* relief or happiness? If so, you may be surprised to learn that there are actually two kinds of prayer, and the kind that most of us practice is actually the *least* effective. Here's what you will discover when you open *The Lost Secrets of Prayer*:

- Seven silent prayers that will turn your life around

- The purpose of true prayer

- How to touch the timeless truth

- The secret power in practicing ceaseless prayer

- How to make all of life be just for you

- The best prayer of any kind

- How to get more from the universe than you ask for

- The real danger of wasted energies

- How to develop the unconquerable self in you

- Why you cannot see the Higher Intelligence within yourself

- 125 special insights to aid your personal inner work

1-56718-276-3; 240 pp., 5¼ x 8   **$9.95**

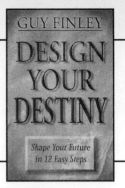

Design Your Destiny

Shape Your Future in 12 Easy Steps

Guy Finley

These twelve powerful inner life exercises will help you master the strong and subtle forces that actually determine your life choices and your destiny. You'll discover why so many of your daily choices up to now have been made by default, and how embracing the truth about yourself will banish your self-defeating behaviors forever. Guy Finley reveals and removes many would-be roadblocks to your inner transformation, telling you how to dismiss fear, cancel self-wrecking resentment, quit secret self-sabotage, and stop blaming others for the way you feel.

After reading *Design Your Destiny*, you'll understand why you are perfectly equal to every task you set for yourself, and that you truly *can* change your life for the better!

- Start your life over again on a higher & happier level
- Erase your fearful feelings once and for all
- Slow down your life and gain new self-command
- Stop being a slave to the painful relationships of your past
- Eliminate unconscious acts of self-sabotage

1-56718-282-8; 216 pp., 5³⁄₁₆ x 8 $9.95

To order, call 1-800-THE MOON

Prices subject to change without notice